Julie Johnson
12294 Cranes Ave.
Richland, MI 49083

RV in NZ

By

Carolyn Harris

How to Spend
Your Winters Freedom
Camping
South – Way South
in
New Zealand

Marble Mountain Press

Cartoons by Ciel Downing

Produced in the USA by Richard Mort & Associates, Portland, Oregon

Library of Congress Control Number: 2003116920

ISBN 0-9748552-0-0

*Address Requests to: Marble Mtn. Press
                       1250 Biddle Rd, F2-217
                       Medford, OR 97504

PREFACE

Small sailboat owners, my husband Dave and I spent several winters varnishing, repairing rusty fittings and leaky water pumps, always checking over our shoulders for that next storm front waiting to rock and roll us. We were ready for a new winter adventure, but it just wasn't going to be near our home in the Shasta Cascade Mountains. We weren't ready to trade the nicked knuckles and salt-crusted feet for frozen fingers and fur-lined boots.

We took a *tiki* tour to New Zealand, found the price was right for our limited retirement income and returned to buy our own *motorcaravan* the following year. We've spent the last six winters zigzagging up and down both islands from Ninety Mile Beach in the North Island (NI) to Bluff in the South Island (SI), stopping to enjoy new friends, taking the scenic route down a lonely golf course or poking around on a back road. If the weather looks bad, we go to the cinema. The best part is, we haven't dragged anchor in our *movan* yet.

INTRODUCTION

Next winter head south for some *freedom camping* in the Land of the Long White Cloud. I don't mean pavement parking in Arizona. I mean south — way south — New Zealand, where *freedom camping* means firing up your *barbe* next to a rugged river, the Tasman Sea or a *reserve* in a small town. There you can enjoy happy hour with a *Kiwi,* a New Zealand citizen, not the hairy brown fruit or the flightless, sightless, nocturnal bird that spends most of its time grubbing in the dirt.

Why that far south? Because New Zealand is in the southern hemisphere. Seasons are reversed. Summer is December to March. Time it right in December and you'll leave on the shortest day of the year and arrive in Auckland, New Zealand the longest day of the year. School holidays are from mid December to the end of January and *Motorcamps* begin filling after *Boxing Day.*

New Zealand is clean green and spectacular. Just how spectacular? Check out *Lord of the Rings* and *The Two Towers* again. *Kiwis* love the outdoors. You'll find boating, fishing, diving, skiing. Almost anything you like to do, you can do in New Zealand, and at a reasonable price. A round of golf? About 3 to 20 $US for green fees.

There are over four hundred courses varying from championship clubs to local courses.

If you enjoy hunting — deer, elk, chamois and wild pig are available. Hunting without a registered guide is not recommended, mainly for your own safety. This is a very rugged country. There is a six week season for game birds, however other *vermin* hunting is not controlled by seasons. If you bring a firearm, it MUST be registered with the police.

Also a plus — no creepy crawly poisonous critters. There is a rarely seen poisonous spider, but you can slosh through the mangroves or plunk down in the *bush* without checking first for an unfriendly resident.

I've covered the where, when and why. This book covers the how. This isn't a travel guide trying to wow you with tourist delights or a *How to Live in New Zealand on a Dollar a Day*. I will take you on a *tiki tour* and if you're still interested, I'll show you step by step *How to Buy a Motorcaravan and Spend Three to Four Months Each Winter south — way south.*

TABLE OF CONTENTS

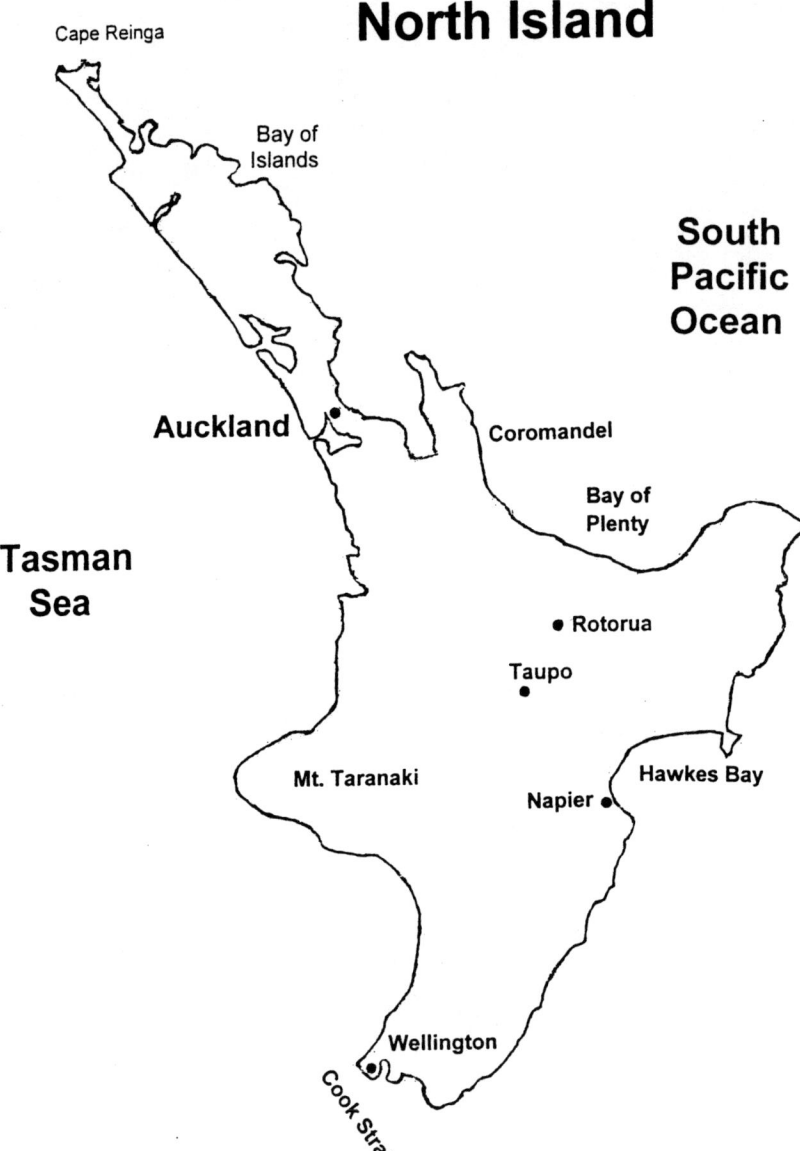

North Island

Cape Reinga

Bay of
Islands

South
Pacific
Ocean

Auckland

Coromandel

Bay of
Plenty

Tasman
Sea

Rotorua

Taupo

Mt. Taranaki

Hawkes Bay

Napier

Wellington

Cook Strait

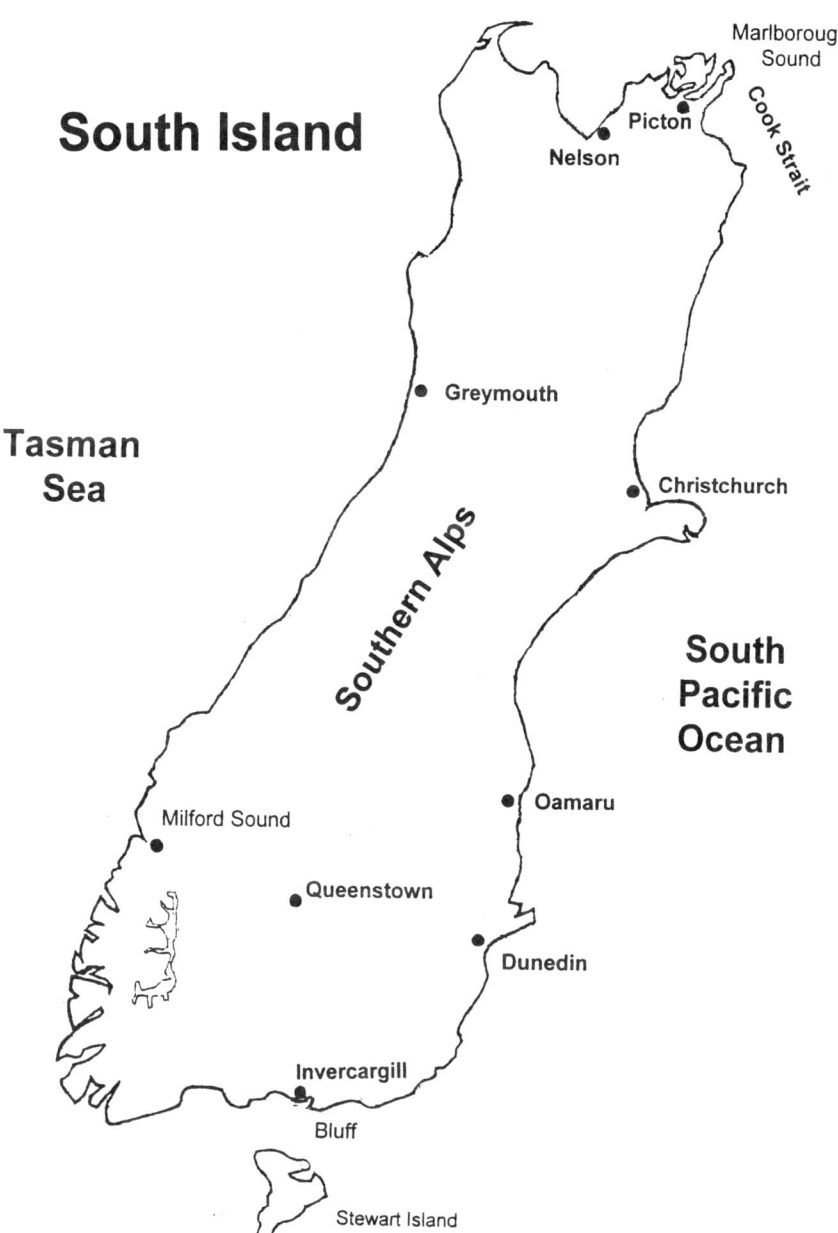

South Island

Tasman
Sea

Marlborough
Sound

Cook Strait

Picton

Nelson

Greymouth

Christchurch

Southern Alps

South
Pacific
Ocean

Milford Sound

Oamaru

Queenstown

Dunedin

Invercargill

Bluff

Stewart Island

The Treaty House, Waitangi National Reserve (NI)
The Treaty of Waitangi was signed in 1840 between
the Maori and Representatives of Queen Victoria.
It's never been ratified, and they're still
trying to figure out what it means.

LET'S TRY A TIKI TOUR

How will you get there? It's a twelve hour flight from Los Angeles International Airport. We like to take an early evening flight, settle in with dinner and a couple of movies, then sleep, well — pretend to sleep. An early evening flight will arrive in Auckland, New Zealand early morning. Clear customs, change some money, pick up your rental car and you're ready to start the day.

You'll need a passport and a round trip ticket. If you plan to stay more than ninety days, you'll need a visa. Obtaining a visa is a simple procedure. Send your passport to your local New Zealand Consulate (ours is in Los Angeles) with a copy of your round trip ticket and proof of enough income you won't go on the *dole*. A credit card statement with available credit or a copy of your retirement income will work.

You'll need to provide return postage, and I always request a delivery receipt since I get a little paranoid about my passport — I don't want to lose that lovely photo. The New Zealand Consulate will stamp the visa in the back of your passport and return it within a week. If you have questions, contact them by phone (you'll get a real person) or www.immigration.gov.nz. If you're working with a travel agent, they usually handle all your documentation.

New Zealand is three long narrow islands, laying more or less north-south for one thousand miles, with hundreds of tiny islands scattered like paint specks, and some available only to birds and the *Department of Conservation (DOC)*.

The North Island, the second largest in area, has the largest population. The larger South Island has fewer people than Auckland alone. Stewart Island, the smallest and coldest is said to be a good place to *tramp*. I wouldn't know. The closest we got was Bluff, the jumping off point for the ferry, where we spent three days wedged up against a cement block *toilet* hoping our *movan* wouldn't blow over.

New Zealand temperatures range from sub-tropical in the north to temperate in the south. The main mountain ranges are a barrier to the prevailing westerly winds causing higher rainfall in the west. Remember, New Zealand is reversed — warm northerlies come from the north and southerlies blow in from the Antarctic.

Auckland, the largest city with the only international airport is about two thirds of the way up the North Island. Four hours north of Auckland is the Bay of Islands where the Cream Boat meanders through the islands dropping off supplies, newspapers and passengers to homes and summer *bachs* and *cribs*.

White Island is an active volcano off the east coast of

the north island. A tourist boat departs daily from Whakatane. You're provided with a hard hat to explore the remains of the old sulfur mill and pick your way with a guide through the steaming vents to the mouth of the bubbling crater with instructions to "Duck behind a rock, don't run for the boat, if it explodes."

Down the ladder from the Pelorus Mail Boat (SI)

About eight hours south of Auckland at Wellington, *The Interislander* links the north and south islands. Cars, trucks and motor caravans ride below, and passengers are outside on the deck or in one of the lounges. Ferries cross the sometimes very rough Cook Strait, then nose their way

3

into Marlboro Sounds to Picton, a small town on the north end of the South Island.

Nearby at Havelock, a mail boat takes tourists, supplies and passengers through mussel farms and more islands. Occasionally, a ladder is lowered off the bow into the not-too-warm water and a laughing passenger departs, wading ashore suitcase over his head. Fortunately, *Kiwis* have a sense of humor and the ability to laugh at themselves. If you're averse to getting wet, stay on the boat and stay off the jet boats in Queenstown where they zoom up the Shotover River for a white knuckle ride. If you don't get wet, you haven't gotten your money's worth.

Christchurch, the third large city (very English) is about five hours down the east coast of the South Island. You're either going to go down the west coast or the east coast of the South Island, even in the summer. The Southern Alps squash up out of the middle of the South Island and sandwich the west coast between the Alps and the Tasman Sea.

This west coast of the South Island is one of the most beautiful areas of New Zealand. Although a road connects Christchurch to Greymouth, a round trip on the *Trans Tasman Railroad* through Arthur's pass takes a day. It's a better way to see the scenery, not the road.

On a two week *tiki tour,* you can fly into Auckland, rent a car or a *motorcaravan*, spend a day or two, then check out the Bay of Islands, drop south again and head west through the Waitomo Glow Worm Caves, or east and spend time in Napier, the Art Deco Town. Farther south, free tours of parliament are available in windy Wellington where you'll catch *The Interislander* across the Cook Strait to the South Island, probably dropping off your rental car and picking up a new one in Picton.

In that two week time frame, you can slip down the west coast of the South Island and cross back into Queenstown, the adventure capitol of New Zealand, about two thirds of the way down the Southern Alps, then cut back up to Christchurch and have time for that train ride back across the Southern Alps to Greymouth or a quick trip out to Akaroa, a French settlement. In Christchurch, you'll probably end your *tiki tour,* drop off your car or *motorcaravan* and head back to Auckland.

If you're a little nervous about your first *tiki tour*, your travel agent can book your accommodations, have your rental car ready, and book your *Tranzrail* ferry passage.

Warning: Book your ferry passage in advance at www.interisland.co.nz
If you're afraid of sheep, don't visit New Zealand

GETTING AROUND

In New Zealand —
> You will get wet.
> You will get fat.
> You will get lost.

I can't help you much with the first two. Wear old shoes and a waterproof hairdo — and bring a bigger pair of pants with an elastic waist.

The first step in the *Let's not get lost again today* problem is to get a map. If you're renting a van or car, they'll give you one to get you out of town. Most towns have easily located *Tourist Information Centers* which have free maps.

The most specific maps are Jasons Route Planners which cover smaller areas and point out major attractions, *Tourist Information Centers*, and walking *tracks* which I'll cover later. The Top Ten Holiday Parks and HAPNZ Holiday Accomodation Parks provide free touring maps with directions to their next park. Each town will also have a free local map. Just ask at the Information Center.

If you're a member of AAA in the US, bring your card. All privileges are reciprocal with The *New Zealand Automobile Association* (AA). I carry AA New Zealand towing insurance. When I walked off and left my old truck with its lights on in Medford, Oregon, I called up and said I had a *New Zealand Automobile Association* card, didn't have it with me and didn't know the number. They called New Zealand, verified my membership and had me running and out of there within twenty minutes. If I sound like I'm pushing AAA, I want to say up front I'm not a member and don't even know who my local rep is.

Your AAA towing card will cover towing your own New Zealand vehicle. It will get you discounts on motels and entertainment, and best of all get you free maps not available to the public that show the back roads. You'll need these for *freedom parking*. Check out AAA's sister at *www.nzaa.co.nz*.

Even with a map, you'll get lost. You can't rely on the sun — it's in the wrong place, and even if you know where you're going, there's no warning when you get there — just tiny signs you can maybe read as you're going past with a truck on your tail. And only the cross streets are marked, so you're never sure which street you're driving on.

We wandered around an Auckland suburb one day looking for a business. The 800 block was on one side, the 300 on the other. And, six streets can converge in a spoke and come out the other side with a different name. The maps are a trick to read. Papakura. Papamoa. Papatoe-toe. Te Anau. Te Aroho. Te Awamutu. Paraparaumu. Parapara. Parakai. "What road are we looking for? Para — something. There it is! We just passed it, I think."

New Zealand has an unique giveway rule. Check this one out before trying it. Roundabouts are easy. Just remember to always give way to the right. Get yourself in there and keep going round and round till the navigator figures out which exit you want — or you run out of gas.

One-way bridges are a snap, too. If the thick arrow on the sign points the direction you're headed, you have the right of way. In the South Island, you share very high one-way bridges with a train. Your first trip over a deep gorge clicking along straddling the rails with only more rails in sight, hoping the engineer knows what he's doing, will be just as memorable as your first bunji jump.

One-way bridge. Dark black arrow means oncoming traffic has the right-of-way.

You'll probably fly into Auckland International Airport south of Auckland. Not the easiest place to face your first time driving on the left side of the road in a strange vehicle that flips on the windshield wipers and smears bugs every time you reach for your turn signals.

If you're heading north, time your trip to avoid commuter traffic. The *motorway* cuts through downtown Auckland, then jams all the traffic across a narrow bridge into North Shore. Road construction which has gone on for several years adds to the confusion.

Traveling around Auckland can be enough to start your holiday off with a friendly fight. Just because you find an off ramp, don't expect an on ramp to be nearby. It's like picking your way through a maze to get back up on the *motorway*. We spent part of an otherwise pleasant afternoon driving back and forth under the *motorway* with, "Not that road, we tried that one before."

After six years, we can find our way around Auckland, but don't unless absolutely necessary. Finding a parking place for a car, let alone a *motorcaravan,* is almost impossible. If you want to tour Auckland and have a *motorcaravan*, stay at Manukau Top 10 Holiday Park in Manukau City. It's close to the airport, near a shopping mall, and the local buses stop right out front.

> **Warning**: Avoid the one-eyed Taniwha, a distant cousin of the Loc Ness Monster. He hangs out south of Auckland near the *motorway* at Meremere.

EAT DRINK AND GET FAT

Remember my warning about getting fat! You can find Indian, Thai and Chinese restaurants. Just about anything you find at home. New Zealand is short on Mexican restaurants, but they can be found. English buffets are often loaded with mutton, cream, and fancy pastries.

KFC, McDonald's and Burger King taste pretty much like home, but pizzas have lost something in the translation. Ever try spaghetti on pizza? Me neither. There's a Denny's behind the large cinema in Manukau City. Funny, I don't get cravings for a Denny's meal at home, but near the end of my four month stay, I start thinking more and more about that Breakfast Skillet.

Larger towns have supermarkets with bakeries and delis. You'll need your *trolly* or *trundler.* Smaller towns have *butcheries*, bakeries, *dairies* and *milk bars.*

Most food is cheap when the exchange rate is figured in. Over the last six years, the $US has fluctuated from .65 to .45 $NZ. French bread is about 1.40 $NZ — figure about seventy cents US. Fruits and *vegges* are cheap and abundant in their summer. Blackberries, raspberries, *strawbs, capsicuns, cougarettes, butternut, silverbeet,* and *marrow* are in season. A large bunch of supermarket asparagus runs about 1 $NZ. Avocados are as low as five for 1 $NZ at the *greengrocer* or on a table in someone's yard. Just pick the ones you want and drop your money in an *honesty box. Swedes* are 2 $NZ per bag — Dave's a Swede, *in good nick,* too, but he won't fit in a bag. Fruits and *vegges* are more expensive in the South Island. Hawks Bay and the Northland near Kiri Kiri are good produce areas. In March, the first crop of apples from the South Island hits the markets as low as 2 $NZ per bag.

Meat is fresh and cheap. Most cuts are the same as US cuts, but watch the T-bones — the butcher steals the fillet. Hungry for a hamburger on that new *barbe?* Better ask for *steak mince* or you might end up with *beetroot* in that patty. Or try a *banger* — good with onions. Of course not as good as Wisconsin *bangers* my traveling Wisconsin food expert tells me. Watch the *hogget,* too. It's one-year-old lamb, not pork. The beef seems a little gamier — possibly fresher.

If you like sea food, try tuna, snapper, mahi mahi or salmon. Dig your own *tua tua* or *pipi* or find some *Paua,* a little smaller than California abalone, but the price is right — our neighbors give them to us. Supermarkets carry good supplies of sea food if you don't want to get your toes sandy.

New Zealand is VERY careful about agricultural disease. When clearing customs, you're asked if you've been on a farm or golf course in the last thirty days. Golf shoes need to be disinfected. Their economy would be devastated if any of the European or Asian diseases got into the country. We eat a lot of lamb in New Zealand. Masterfoods, a New Zealand company, has a good mint jelly — worth sticking a few extra jars in your suitcase.

Chook is often for company dinners. Not long ago, it was the most expensive meat in *Godzone*. Deer and elk are raised for the export market. It can be found in the upscale markets like Big Fresh or on the menu in some restaurants.

New Zealand is dairy country and heavy on milk and cream. Breakfast cream for cereal has the texture of unwhipped whipping cream. There's Cream # 1 and Cream # 2. We finally settled on plain milk for our cereal — American cereal. Olivani makes a good olive oil-based margarine and American brand margarine, produced in Australia, is available. You'll find Paul Newman dressings, produced in Australia, and that's one the Australians improved on. Better than you can buy here and at a cheaper price, too. If you want American cranberry juice, it's *dear*.

Lemon & Paeroa, a lemon flavored mineral water, Coca Cola, Pepsi, various sodas, and Ch'i Water — New Zealand herbal mineral water in the green bottle — is available. I go through a bottle of Ch'i water a day. Dave can't stand it.

Beer and wine are sold in supermarkets. Try Cheep Liquor or Liquorland for hard liquor. Many Kiwis make their own moonshine. Home manufacture is allowed in small quantities. Moonshine Kits are available in stores. The main government concern seems to be do it right, don't kill yourself. Though the *Kiwi* government looks kindly on moonshiners, they turn the evil eye on pot growers. We've shared moonshine — some excellent, some passable, but we've never been offered pot. We hang around with an older crowd. If they smoke, they don't brag.

There are nice little delis, bakeries, and espresso cafes in any town. A *Kiwi* favorite is meat pie, a flaky, high calorie meat pie. Beware, unless you brought those elastic pants.

Hangi in the Bay of Islands (NI)

You will want to try a traditional *hangi* at least once during your visit. Stones are placed in a lighted fire pit, then lamb, pork or chicken, and *kamara*, and *vegges* wrapped in muslin are wedged into wire frames and lowered over the hot stones. The meal gets more than a dash of water — they use buckets. This steaming pile is covered with fresh dirt. Your *hangi* takes a while to cook, so there's time for a long happy hour. Enjoy a *hangi* along with *Maori* singing and dancing at Rotorua (NI). At an *EBOP* rally, we had chicken and wild pig. East Cape is known for its wild pig hunting. (If you're a REAL pig hunter, you don't use a gun — you chase them down with a knife.)

> **Warning**: If you buy New Zealand cereal — throw away the cereal. Eat the Box.
> If you want a *Swede*, find one *in good nick*.

WHERE TO STAY

Unless you've somehow managed to buy a *motor-caravan* sight unseen — it's done, we've met people who have purchased through individuals and dealers and seemed happy — you'll probably need accommodations for a night or two while you shop around.

Motels are reasonably priced once you get away from the airport. The Great South Road runs parallel to and crosses over the *motorway*. Grocery stores, restaurants and motels are all along this old highway. Fifteen to twenty minutes south at Manurewa or Papakura, traffic thins out and prices are reasonable — don't forget your AAA card. Stop at a supermarket for breakfast and snacks. Rooms have mini kitchens with coffee and tea. And don't get stuffy if the elderly gentleman at the desk asks, *"Can I knock you up in the morning?"*

Papakura is the home of the *New Zealand Motorcaravan Association* — NZMCA. I'll cover this organization later, but it's right off the Great South Road and you'll want to stop in, get your membership and have them explain the benefits.

Even if you've brought your own linen, you probably won't want to be digging through your luggage after a twelve hour flight from Los Angeles. But another alternative is to book into a Holiday Park. The nearest one at Manukau City is close to downtown Auckland, a mall and Rainbow's End Adventure Park — a large amusement park.

Holiday motorcamps are Top 10 and HAPNZ. Top 10 parks are usually a little larger. They spend more on advertising and seem to pull in more tourist trade–rental vans. HAPNZ park owners — some are *council* owned, are uncrowded and usually Mom and Pop run with local residents living on site in permanent *caravans* with their flowers, pets and kids. If you hear, "puss, puss, puss" under your window, someone's looking for his *moggy*.

Motorparks are clean and friendly. We've had few problems other than the time Dave was in the shower in a rural area of the Northland and the caretaker in a hurry to get out fishing, hosed him down with a firehose.

Rooms are rented with or without linen, at a lower price. They can be cabins with cooking facilities to backpacker accommodations — several to a room. No linen. Back-packers, usually younger and international, often have their own hotels. These are listed in the backpacker magazines and newspapers.

Though you won't be sharing a room with a backpacker, you'll share toilet/shower facilities, the community kitchen and TV/ reading room if you don't have your own cooking facilities or want to watch the evening news and don't have a TV.

Caravans are also available for rent. Old, often up on blocks with flowers around them. Always ask to check them out ahead of time if you have any doubts.

Of course, there are fancy hotels around the airport and downtown Auckland, and Bed and Breakfast and Pub Stays. Just don't book a room right over the pub if you're looking for sleep.

I'll cover freedom and low cost camping later, once you're settled in your own *movan*.

I've talked about AAA discounts. If you have a KOA card, bring it, too. Top 10 parks offer a 10% discount with your KOA card. They sell their own card for 20 $NZ (about 10 $US). The card, purchased when you check in, is good for two years and is reciprocal with a KOA card. It offers discounts on entertainment and food. For more information, see www.topparks.co.nz. HAPNZ offers their own discount card, also. Check www.holidayparks.co.nz.

You'll be asked, "Are you Canadian?" Seems we all look alike and talk alike, but the Canadians can be insulted if mistaken for an American. I travel with a *Cheesehead*, the Wisconsin species, not a Dutchman. My best friend is a *Dallie*, not the spotted species. We often travel with *Poms* but never with *hoons*.

> **Warning**: Don't leave home without your AAA and KOA card.
> Avoid a *motorcamp* across the river from a lonely bull elk.

5

A DAY AHEAD AND
A DOLLAR SHORT

New Zealand is a day ahead. And the dates are backward. March first is 1-3.

This is as good a place as any to mention the New Zealand Herald. News is hard to come by if you don't have a TV. Radio news is available, but if you're traveling, stations fade in and out. Just about the time you figure out the local station news schedule, you're out of range.

The New Zealand Herald is almost impossible to find in the South Island and in beach towns. If you buy a copy, pass it along at a campground. It's always appreciated. Even got us a free drink one time. The Herald is available at supermarkets, bookstores and BP Stations. It may sell out early in the day. It isn't the best source for news.

You have to pick between the "Oh Poor Lady," "She Had her Benefit Cut," "American Billionaire Caught Smuggling Pot and Buys Way Out," "Local *MP* Has Tummy Tuck" and "Beware of the Mauler," a little stingy thing that bites you on the *bum* at the Mt. Maunganui beach, to find out what's going on in the world. Check the

Herald out at www.herald.co.nz.

When you move south, Wellington has its own paper — more politically oriented since it's published in the capitol. Christchurch and Dunedin have their own newspapers. You probably won't have time for Dunedin on a *tiki tour*. There are area and local papers, many free and a good way to find out if there are car races nearby, what's on at the cinema or where the restaurants are located. Rotary Clubs, Lions Clubs, Country Western Music Clubs — whatever you're affiliated with at home, you'll probably find listed. Just show up. *Kiwis* will be glad to meet you. Organizations you might not find at home are listed, too. We spent an afternoon in Taupo watching the finals of the Ladies Marching Teams — very professional military-style drill teams.

You can also buy a Herald at the New Zealand Post. Look for the flag. The Post Office is sometimes located at a counter in the back of a store. The New Zealand Post provides and processes forms for the *Land Transport Safety* — similar to our Department of Motor Vehicles. You can file a Certificate of non-operation when you store your *motorcaravan* or pay your *diesel mileage tax*, covered in Chapter VII. You can buy a prepaid envelope to send to NZMCA when you want your mail forwarded, and send and receive mail.

Your US Dollar won't even buy you a smile in New Zealand. Bank of New Zealand has a money exchange counter next to the rental car counter in the Auckland Airport. They pay the going exchange rate minus a service transaction fee.

Tipping is not expected in New Zealand, but you'll

want some cash in your pocket. BP and Shell stations are prevalent. Your US BP and Shell card won't work in New Zealand, but any Mastercard or Visa buys gas, entertainment or food. It's almost impossible to figure the exact cost as the exchange rate and fees will appear when the financial transaction hits your account and you can't predict the exchange rate in advance.

You will want to use your credit card for money advances if you're staying over a period of months. Bring at least one extra card in case there's a mix up on your primary card and of course you've listed and tucked away your card numbers along with your passport number and other necessary information in case they disappear. It's also a good idea to call your card company in advance and let them know your travel plans so they don't assume the card is stolen and is piling up fees in some exotic location.

Even that can cause a mix-up. I notified my card company in advance but a tire shop spelled my name wrong causing a flag on the account. When I tried to withdraw cash at a New Zealand bank, I was told the card was invalid. The New Zealand bank couldn't connect me with my card company and I had to walk two blocks, find a coin phone and call collect.

New Zealand pay phones are coin and card phones. You need a prepaid card to operate a card phone. The problem was straightened out, but always expect a problem and you won't be disappointed. For a cash advance on your credit card, carry your passport. Some banks require it but others just check a drivers license.

Buying a cashiers check is almost impossible. My *motorcaravan* insurance comes due in February each year

— usually when I'm pretty far from Papakura. I don't want to send cash through the mail. The explanation I was given for not being able to purchase a cashiers check was, "We're afraid of drug transactions." Seems pretty far-fetched that my insurance agent is a drug dealer.

I had a check from a New Zealand business for a Mini Cooper I'd sold. When I tried to cash the check, I was told the same thing, "You can't cash the check without an account because we're afraid of drug transactions." I finally took the check and opened a savings account, which gradually dwindled as the fees ate into the principle. The account did give me an ATM card, though — my backup if I don't plan ahead. There're LOTS of bank holidays in New Zealand. It's easy to get caught short of cash. And, to add to the confusion, one bank may take a local holiday and another 20 kilometers away will be open.

The only kind thing I can say about the New Zealand Banking System — the tellers are friendly and always smile when they say, "Sorry."

National Holidays
New Year's Day: January 1
Waitangi Day: February 6
Good Friday and Easter Monday: Late March
    or early April
Anzac Day: April 25
Queen's Birthday: first Monday of June
Labour Day: fourth Monday of October
Christmas Day: December 25
Boxing Day: December 26

Warning: Bank holidays sneak up on you when you're cash poor.
Better watch out for that Mauler, too.

6

LET'S BUY A MOVAN

You've stayed with me this far. Are you ready to *have a go* on your own *movan*? *Yeah! Well, good on you.*

If you took a *tiki tour* before this step and thought you'd rather rent a *movan* and snoop around a little first, there were two or three ways to rent, through Britz, Maui or Adventure, through a dealer or through a private individual. You might have even exchanged your RV with a *Kiwi*.

The major rental companies have counters in or near the airport — hop off the plane, hop in a *movan*. Dealers and individuals can be located anywhere. Get there, meet some nice people and hop in. A trade can be arranged through the New Zealand Motor Caravan Association (NZMCA). Advertise and work it out. Just make sure they don't hand you a bucket.

The first year we rented a Maui *motorcaravan* and I was afraid to ask, "Why the bucket?" It wasn't as bad as I thought. All toilets are cassette type. It's the grey water that can be a problem. Most of the rentals are self-contained now, although in 2003 there were still a few 'bucket vans' around. NZMCA encourages self-containment and provides free certification by approved members.

There are many ways to buy a *movan*. I can't imagine a *Kiwi* being anything but honest and I've met people who purchased *movans* sight unseen over the internet and seemed pleased. We purchased ours through a dealer. Dealers are located in most *cities* and have web sites you can browse to get you started. NZMCA's *Codes of Construction* and *Handy Hints* cover your technical questions.

Size matters when buying a *movan*. Bigger isn't always better. When we bought our 3.2 meter high 7 meter long (including the *boot*) *movan* in 1995, it was considered large. Lately, we're seeing more and more big bus conversions on the road.

Though Dave is an excellent driver, the first year we banged the cab top on a low hanging tree branch pulling into a parking space in town. Now, I always jump out and guide him in. Store canopies stick out over parking spaces and trees are trimmed for cars, not *movans*. Length is not a problem. A lot of parking is nose-in parking with enough room to back out without blocking traffic. Width is a problem. One-way bridges are narrow, with cement curbs that come up high enough to snag our fold-down metal stairs at least once a year. Friends who have a small bus conversion catch their front *mudguard* — buses are lower to the ground. We carry a crowbar and pry our stairs back in place.

Signs stick out in parking areas high enough to clear a car, but not a *movan*. We hit Santa Claus and tore off his arm. Not the best way to make friends in a small town. Don't cut corners too tight either or you might end up with a street sign in your bed. And watch for *judder bars*. Don't *go like the clappers*.

We picked a *movan* with a 3.2 meter height so we could sit up in bed. We also have a roof vent for added ventilation at night. Most Class C cabovers are so tight they end up as a catch all. They're usually unvented, have small side windows and are hard to get in and out of when you get older. I'm a night owl and Dave's up with the *chooks* so we needed enough space to go about our own schedules. *Movan* length is pretty standard, 2.6 to 3.2 meters. We have a *boot* in the back to carry a table and chairs, a *barbe,* and a hose. We travel anywhere we choose from downtown Auckland to *freedom camping* in the *bush*.

If you want to go bigger and have the *big bickies*, contact Robert Baillie at Vanco www.vanconz@ihug.co.nz. They'll custom design and build whatever you want. They're back- loaded with orders, so just make sure you plan a season ahead. Their larger tour bus conversions are usually for people who sell their homes and become permanent vagabonds. *Licence Classes* are based on type and weight of the vehicle. Vehicles over 3500 kg need a Certificate of Loading. These larger *motorcaravans* move around less, haul a tow car and spend more time in larger *motorcamps* such as DeBretts. They also show up at *rallies*, but are seldom spotted *freedom camping*, maybe because they stay on *sealed* roads and don't want them dusty and nicked from the *metal* roads.

Vanco and CR Monroe, both located in the North Island are two of the top caravan converters for the average size *motorcaravan*. We've done business with both. Other companies are listed in NZMCA but it would be best to avoid a *one off* homebrew. You might be buying the bugs they've worked out and won't repeat on their next conversion. If you decide to have a van conversion, you'll have no problems working out plans, prices or any problem by E-mail, fax or phone. Most *Kiwis* won't *diddle you.* They put a high value on honesty and integrity.

front door was removed and a new one built in the middle allowing two people to sit in the front while moving. To the left of the door is a flip-down barbe. When complete, it will be similar to US models.

A secondhand *movan* is the most economical way to go. We bought our 1990 Class C Ford Trader, CR Monroe conversion in 1995 from Ron Neil Motors in Auckland. In 2003 we had it appraised by an *Independent Valuer* for 35 $NZ. The *valuer* told us older vans are usually priced at the same or higher purchase value because of the high cost of new conversions. New Zealand has a high *GST* and everything is built more or less from scratch. In 2003, our *movan* was appraised for the same amount we'd paid in 1995.

There are a few new imports available. We checked out Italian imports in Lake Taupo. They were nice looking but twice the price and less space than most comparable vans. There are also a few — very few — US models with right-hand steering around. They're brought in usually by *Kiwi* owners who traveled in the US.

The main type of conversions are Japanese buses or Class C's built on a Ford Trader, Nissan or Mitsubishi chassis. There are some Mercedes.

Japanese buses are low and narrow. Sometimes the roofs are raised for more headroom. The narrow width limits the floor plan, especially when the floor is not always the same level. Step up around the door entry and try not to fall down the hole in the middle of the night. We have been told you can't rely on the odometers. The Japanese often roll back the odometers before exporting them to New Zealand. Once in New Zealand, odometer readings are tracked on registration and *road user fees*.

Some *Kiwis* with joint problems prefer a bus conversion so they don't have to climb up and down a ladder. With Class C's, watch the cab-over headroom or it's wasted space.

You'll still have a step-up space on the floor, but it doesn't protrude into the walking plan.

Diesel is the fuel of choice. *Petrol* is expensive and measured in litres. Fortunately, you don't have far to go. Two to three hours can usually get you to a whole new district. Remember, don't ask for *gas* — you might get some. In August, 2003, the New Zealand government introduced a "flatulence tax" on sheep and cattle to help fund research into global warming. Local protesting farmers dubbed it the "Fight Against Ridiculous Taxes" (FART). And we think we corner the market on nutty politicians?

Floor plan layout will make all the difference in whether you're stepping over each other. You'll still be stuck with a one *fanny* — sorry about that, I meant a one *bum* kitchen. If you picked out a really small van, you'll only have a bed which slides into a sofa, a sink, a small cooking appliance and maybe a very small potty. A Class C sleeps 4-6 people.

The ex-Maui and Britz rentals are designed to jam in people for short vacations. Maui Direct recycles its vans through dealers. Be aware these have been rental vehicles and don't have much in the way of interior comforts. One bed is usually the dining area — a tight U shaped affair about as comfortable as a restaurant booth. In our rental van we stood on the stove to get into bed.

If you're going to spend winters, plan sleeping space for yourself and perhaps an occasional guest who can always be moved outside if he snores.

We bought a Class C layout floor plan. On entering, remember the steering is on the right and unit entry will be on the curbside or left. Our sofa, eating area is to the left with kitchen and bathroom to the right. Most have the dining area on the right under the large rear window.

One owner complained he didn't like his dining table under the window because when he pulled into a site, people passing could see what he was eating. We eat outside as much as possible and people can look all they want. If you have bad eating habits, consider tinted windows. He didn't say why he didn't just back into the site. Most have bushes or some barrier around them.

We preferred the Class C layout because it feels bigger and it's more open. We're both readers and each have our own sofa. After a hard day of walking the beach, visiting with neighbors or reading a few chapters, we're *clapped out* and need a nap. Two sofas work just fine — they're twin bed size so they double as beds for company. The downside of this — we don't have a walk through. We have a bench seat in the cab.

When the *loo* door bangs and we can't stop and I have to get to the rear, or when we're surrounded by sheep on the road, can't move and I need the camera, I have to slide over the seatback like a fat seal, grab the camera and squeeze back in without kicking Dave in the head. With other layouts, you have bucket seats and can step into the unit if you forget a map or need another cup of coffee. It's a trade off. Check out all floor plans and see what suits you best.

Your new *movan* will need a current *Warrant of Electrical Fitness*. It's good for four years. New Zealand electrical power is 230 volt, 50 cycle. A certified official will check switches, *hot points*, mains and anything else electrical in your *movan*. *Hot points* have switches but they're reversed. ON points downward (because we're below the equator?).

You'll need *globes*, usually with a bayonet base, for your 230, 12 volt fixtures and *torches*. We have some unusual size *globes* and pack the burned-out sample to the *lamp shop* and try to keep a spare on hand. They're hard to find in small towns.

Bathrooms (*loos*) are self-contained. I keep calling ours the bathroom — old habits are hard to break. If we had a flood, we might have a bathroom. Don't bring soap to the *baths* either, just your bathing *togs*. All *loos* have a cassette toilet — easy to use. In an emergency, they can even be dumped in a regular toilet.

Any brand of toilet paper will work in your cassette toilet. Most toilet paper in New Zealand has the texture of the *New Zealand Herald*. If you have a tender *bum,* buy a softer brand from the *chemist*. Wrappings read, "This roll is the property of the New Zealand Government." *Kiwis* do a lot of recycling (maybe we're supposed to recycle?).

Cassette toilets last two people three to four days. A self-contained unit has a holding tank for grey water which is dumped pretty much like US rigs. There are different sized tanks. Capacities will be listed on your self-containment certificate. Don't buy a *movan* without a self-containment certificate. Self-containment will not be an option in the future and you're not welcome to *freedom camp* in many areas without self-containment.

Dump sites are available almost anywhere, BP Stations, *motorcamps*, public municipalities. They are clean, maintained and an easy place to dump the old and fill up with fresh water. The NZMCA Handbook lists the locations and I usually mark them on a local map so I can find them from year to year.

Our bathroom sink is a flip down model — it drops down over the toilet. Don't get a flip down model — the drain leaks. It would probably drain right if we always parked level or tilted to the right, but when we raise it back into place, it drips. All over the toilet. No particular problem, just a mess.

The shower on the opposite side drains into the stainless steel floor. We keep a rug on the floor when not showering. Ever step on a cold stainless steel floor in the middle of the night? Newer model sinks are available, and ours would be no problem with one of those small head-only English sinks mounted under the shower head.

Cooking area depends on *bench* space. Our Class C design has a long *bench* under the rear window and a stainless steel sink-drainboard to the right; next to that a two burner stove and oven with a microwave above; then more *bench* space with a leaded glass dish cupboard above and storage drawers below. (By the way, talking to a *Kiwi*, next does not mean next. It's the one after next. Next Sunday isn't the one coming up, but the following week)

Four burner stoves are available but we seldom use more than two burners, have an electric frying pan and use the *barbe*. LPG heated hot water is on demand — noisy but efficient. Hot water heaters in newer models are quieter and built-in under the *benches*. Our neighbor's new hot water heater malfunctions one night, draining all their cold water, too.

We carry drinking water in litre soda bottles. Just an

old habit. Even with a water purifier, I always wonder what's crawling around down in my tanks. I told you there's no poisonous bugs or snakes in New Zealand. There are spiders. Pesky little devils that build webs as fast as you can brush them away. And *mozzies,* particularly in the South Island.

Our three way Electrolux refrigerator is usually on LPG and works fine. I keep frozen meat, ice cream and *ice blocks.* I defrost it every couple of weeks with a hair dryer. The vents need to be kept clean — those pesky little spiders like a warm bed. On a hot day, plan ahead when parking and keep the frig side in the shade.

Occasionally when refrigerators are stored, they develop an air bubble and need to be burped. If this happens, they're taken out and turned upside down. We had a bubble and the flame went out every two or three days. We finally bounced the bubble out on a *metal* road. There's no way you're going to get your frig out of the rig by yourself. They're installed and the unit finished around them. They won't fit through the door even with the trim removed. If you're replacing one, the dealer will take it in and out the window.

Our wardrobe is over the refrigerator next to the bathroom door. The heat from the vent gives me a good place to dry clothes. Drying clothes can be a problem. We do laundry when we're in a *motorcamp* for 2 $NZ a wash load.

The dryers are finicky and either don't get clothes dry or cook them. If you run out of coins and they're almost dry, hang them around your van — if you don't mind a pair of shorts hanging in your face. Chances are you'll buy some *pegs* and rig up a clothes line under your awning. *Laundrettes* are available and listed in NZMCA but it's just usually much easier to do a load while you're hanging around a *motorcamp* for a day.

When you decide on a floor plan, figure out your lifestyle. Are you a gourmet cook, happy hostess or a beach bum? Remember, your squatting on an island in the *Roaring Forties*. It rains even in summer. You'll need a place to hide out and just read away the day or watch *telly*.

TV. I'm not quite sure what to say about this. Even with 150 channels on my satellite in the US, I'm not a big TV fan. New Zealand has three TV stations. TV3 is privately owned. News is available — heavy on local issues, very little world news. "Shock and awe" best describes the news casts. When *Coronation Street* comes on, New Zealand shuts off. We've been invited to drinks, "after *Coronation Street*." *Freedom parking,* you know when *Coronation Street's* on — the generators come out and the *Kiwis* go in.

We brought a 12 volt US TV and VCR as carry-on luggage. We bought a special antenna from a hard-to-find store in Manukau City, recommended as the best. You see some odd homebrew antennas and occasionally a Camping World crankup. Poles are carried in the *boot* and antennas are hooked up at each stop. We bought our poles, flew our antenna high and proud and tried to get a picture. We even had help adjusting the line of sight and checking the lead in.

New Zealand has their own secret TV code and it's not compatible with US TV's. We could watch the tapes I'd brought from the states, but we never did get our very own *Coronation Street*. The problem was solved when I forgot to lash it down one morning. We went around a corner and it ended in the *bin*. I found out after the *dustman* took our *telly* to the *tip*, we needed an annual license to watch the *telly*.

All commercial sales of TV receivers are reported to the *Public Broadcasting Office*. If you don't buy your license, they can track you down. Lucky for us, our *telly* ended in the *tip*. Sky TV is available, so if you really miss your *telly*, buy a dish.

If you're a man, you're probably muttering, "Why's she going on about bad TV and *Coronation Street*. Tell me what's under the *bonnet* and what I'll probably have to deal with while my lady is laying out the *cheerios* and *biscuits* or some *chippies* for happy hour."

You have a better chance of getting a good used chassis if you check the point of origin, Japanese or whatever, listed on the registration. The *Independent Valuer* will note any rust problems and you'll have to get a *Warrant of Fitness (WOF)* before you can even get your *movan* on the road. During the *WOF* inspection they'll check brakes, headlights and crawl under and check moving parts. Between the two of them, they should spot any problems.

If you're concerned about the engine or transmission, buy a *VT Cover* at the *WOF* office. *Express Cover* for 30 days/2000km or *Elite Cover* for up to 36 months with optional tyre cover. Some units are built on new chassis. New Zealand is a warm moist country — vehicles rust easily. Our *roo bars* need a touch up every couple of years. We buy a cheap brush and a small can of paint then toss the stiff brush in the *bin*.

Dave checks but never changes oil. He doesn't have the tools or a proper place to dump the used oil. He does carry *spanners* and screwdrivers. He changes *headlamps* and carries extra belts in case we break down kilometers from cell phone service. *AA* covers us, but they aren't telepathic. Brakes and batteries are a problem if the rig sits for eight months of the year. We store ours where someone fires it up occasionally and runs it around the *paddock*. Antifreeze needs to be changed every three or four years.

We have two 12 volt Group 27 batteries under the entry step. Our house battery runs three to four days without recharging. Days are long and we don't watch *Coronation Street*.

The outside refrigerator vents were changed from rivets to screws for easier cleaning — remember those spiders. We carried over and Dave installed a new crank-up roof vent and MaxxAir Roof Vent Cover from Camping World for our *loo*. MaxxAir Roof Vents are expensive and not common in New Zealand. They're light weight and come in a box, so I just stuffed our clothes around the vent and hauled the whole thing, box and all, as another suitcase. New Zealand has an island climate. It often rains at night. We were worried about outside height in front and the vent cover adds height. But Class C's slope back and *toilets* are always located in the rear. Makes sense doesn't it? You wouldn't have your *toilet* in the cab.

GST is high and RV supplies, usually imported, are expensive if available. When the roof vent over our bed began leaking, we had it reseated at CI Monroe, the factory converter. Services are cheap. It's the products that are expensive.

The cassette toilet slides out

If you want to hear some *bloody* bad language, hang around Dave trying to relight our LPG refrigerator when we change tanks. We pull the shades, he gets on his hands and knees with a blanket over his head and snaps the switch, and snaps the switch, till he can see the tiny blue flame hidden near the floor. Newer models have the controls on top — a good feature to look for.

The toilet is a slick operation and less cumbersome than the one on our RV at home. It's light enough when full to be carried a reasonable distance. Fresh water is available at all dump sites and campgrounds. We carry our own fresh water hose and keep our tanks and water (soda) bottles topped off. Occasionally, if we're on a steep hard haul over Gentle Annie or into Lake Waikarimona in Te Urawera National Park (Old Man Who Roasted his Privates in the Campfire), we skip the fill so we're hauling a little less weight.

Dave scrounged some scrap lumber for leveling blocks, *6 x 2's*. Necessary for *freedom camping*. He also handles the *barbe*. When writing this section, I tried to pin him down about maintenance problems. He said, "It's easier to maintain than the one at home." Probably because it doesn't have all the fancy bells and whistles.

> **Warning:** Watch those *judder bars* without your hard hat.
> Store canopies can bite.
> Avoid a medical emergency during *Coronation Street*.
> Don't buy a rusty chassis.
> Run if the *movan* owner hands you a bucket.

Don't fall asleep too close to a campfire in Te Urewera National Park.

7

LET'S GET THAT NEW
MOVAN ON THE ROAD

Your new *movan* will have a *Warrent of Fitness (WOF)* if it's under 3500 kgs or *Certificate of Fitness (COF)* if it's over 3500 kgs — Safety Inspections from the *Land Transport Safety Authority* www.ltsa.gov.nz. These Safety Inspections are to ensure your vehicle is safe when on the road. Engine and transmission condition are not checked. *WOFs* or *COFs* are not intended as a pre-purchase assessment. Your Safety Inspection is valid for six months and necessary for registration. It will show *speedo* and *hubo* readings. If you fail the first time through, repairs are made and you return with the *movan* for another inspection.

With your *COF* or *WOF* and proof of purchase, you can apply for a *Certificate of Registration*. Motor caravans are classified by weight and/or age and their use. Yours will be for private use. Your registration will have basic information about the *movan* including CC Rating (weight) and ownership history. Registration can be purchased for six or twelve months. When you return home, file a *Certificate of Non Operation* at a *Vehicle Testing Station* or New Zealand Post. If you don't, you'll be liable for past due registration fees and have to pay for a more expensive and harder to pass Safety Inspection when you renew your registration. Use NZMCA for your New Zealand address. You'll receive your registration in the mail.

You'll pay *Road User Charges* on a diesel powered vehicle. Pay for a couple thousand *K's* to get you started. *Distance License* is purchased in units of 1000 *K's* (621 miles) per unit as measured on your *hubo*. *Hubo* and *speedo* readings will be different. If your vehicle is under 3500 kg, the *speedo* is an approved distance recorder. When you run short, just pop into the New Zealand Post, a BP Truck Stop or an AA office and purchase a few more. They'll pull your account up on the computer. Three *K's* cost 82 $NZ.

Registration, *COF* or *WOF* and *Road User Fee* receipts are placed on the *windscreen* passenger side.

You will want vehicle insurance even though New Zealand has no-fault insurance. We purchase ours through NZMCA's *Group Insurance Scheme* — not as sneaky as it sounds. They'll need the information on your registration. Claim settlement is quick and easy. Coverage allows a new windscreen every year. With *metal* roads, you'll need one. AA towing insurance, if you didn't bring your AAA card, is purchased separately.

You'll need a valid driver's license for your *movan* insurance to be valid. New Zealand has safety problems with Asian student drivers. In February 2003 they considered requiring students and new migrants to "sit driving tests before giving them visas because of the concerns about the standard of Asian drivers." The suggestion was dropped.

A United Nations agreement lets licence holders drive for up to twelve months in New Zealand on their own country's licence and visa versa. United States recognizes the agreement. So, with a current US license, you can drive whatever class vehicle you're licensed to drive in the states. New Zealand has Licence Class 1-5. Class I car licence includes *Gross Laden Weight (GLW)* 4500 kg or less. Most Class C's and small bus conversions are Class I. A larger bus conversion would bounce you over the weight limit and you'd need a Class II. If you think you might need a Class II licence, check with the *Land Transport Safety Authority* www.ltsa.gov.nz.

Vehicle Testing Station at Takanini (NI)

There is an exemption for owners of private camper vans to drive a *GLW* vehicle exceeding 4500 kg on a Class I drivers licence if the laden weight of the *movan* does not exceed 4500 kg. If towing any trailer, the weight of the trailer is added to that of the vehicle. If you have questions about this grey area, contact the *Land Transport Safety Authority*.

Kiwi's are polite and friendly — until they get in a small vehicle. Then watch out! It helps to have a 3500 kg *movan* with a *roo bar*. Truck drivers and other *movaners* stay on their fair share of the road, but watch out for those snappy little sports cars and SUV's. Walking is harder than driving. It's pedestrian beware! Always look right AND left before stepping into the street. Pedestrian crossings are only to line you up so you make a better target. If the cross walk is close to a roundabout, they'll zing around the corner from the right and nail you from the rear. We've tried crossing down traffic from a pregnant *mum* with a stroller. We just made a bigger target. We stood in a fairly large space between parked cars. When the line of traffic stopped to allow a car into a shopping mall, the car behind zipped around almost running over my new shoes. And no way in heaven or *Godzone* would I venture out on New Year's Eve again. It's safer in a pool of sharks with a *bloody* fish tacked to your *bum*.

> **Warning:** Don't forget to file a *Certificate of Non Operation* before you return home. Avoid becoming a smear on a Mini's *windscreen*.

NO SHOES. NO SIIIRT.
COULD BE A PROBLEM.

We kind of bounced into buying our *movan* without really thinking things through. We sold a sailboat and knew it was time for a change. We were getting too old for peeling varnish, rusty fittings and night passages. We packed up the dishes, pots, pans and bedding and jammed them in sail bags and boxes along with our clothing. If you don't have a box of household junk you never got around to hauling off to an OP Shop, don't buy anything. Buy it when you get there.

Bring your meds. Some newer meds are either under different names or not available. If something minor pops up, allergies or sore muscles, talk to the *chemist*. Cataflam, for "painful and inflammatory conditions" has "pharmacist only medicine" on the box. You'll show ID, then receive the medicine after a short discussion about proper use. If something serious does happen, New Zealand has top quality medical facilities.

You won't be hassled for payment, but if you have private coverage, just pay the bill and straighten it out with your insurance carrier when you get home. Medicare won't cover you out of the country. A five day hospital stay cost 200 $US. We asked for a bill and they were surprised. They told us, "Most tourists just stick us with the bills."

New Zealand is a small country with just as many budget problems as we have. Pay your own way.

For vitamins, so you can avoid that trip to the hospital, bring your own if you have a special brand, or buy them in a health food store or *chemist shop*. Worried about cosmetics? Estee Lauder, Elizabeth Arden, Paul Mitchell — all the major brands are available from the *hairdresser* or the *chemist shop*.

I had a tooth fall out of my partial plate. I waited in the waiting room forty five minutes while my plate was repaired, then handed back to me with "does that feel okay?" My dentist at home was unable to spot the 30 $NZ repaired tooth.

Bring some linen and at least two lightweight towels per person — they're easy to jam in a box or duffle bag. With all that thermal activity, many *motorcamps* have mineral spas. Lightweight towels work fine and dry quickly. We didn't want to feel like campers so we used regular bedding. Waterbed garters make it easy for the last person up, always me, to pull from the top and straighten the bedding for the day. New Zealand linen is good quality and moderately priced. Look for sales. We have a summer duvet and an electric blanket. Our first trip to the South Island we unpacked the blanket with "What in the hell's this?" New Zealand electric blankets are BIG heating pads.

Check out Farmers and Briscoes for linen, dishes, or

pots and pans. Unless your appliances are universal, purchase them there — a hair dryer (which doubles as a frig defroster), electric frying pan, toaster, iron. Maybe you're the drip dry type and don't need an iron. Some *motorcamps* have irons, but it's handy to have your own. Warehouse is a discount chain similar to US discount stores. They carry food, clothing, sporting goods and household items.

Cash Converters are high quality second hand stores. Even if you're not buying, check them out. Op Shops have good bargains, too.

Enjoying street musicians at Wellington

No shoes, no shirt, could be a problem. Clothes sizes are different. Most women have a hard enough time finding *bathing togs* they like in the US. Bring at least one bathing suit. Always try clothes on before leaving the store. I spent an interesting afternoon trying to buy a pair of shoes and a bra. New Zealand shoe sizes run larger than US. Bras run 10, 12 and 14. Dave forgot a baseball hat. He bought one labeled "New Zealand Product." Inside it read, "Made in China." Like everywhere else — buyer beware. You'll need *jandals* for the showers and *baths*.

Bring comfortable clothes and shoes. I bring my old gardening shoes, a good pair of walking shoes and a pair for when we go out. *Kiwis* wear *jandals and gumboots* in the rural areas. They won't care a bit what you wear, and even if they did, they'd be too polite to say

Remember, you're tramping around through the *Roaring Forties*. Even in summer, you'll need a jacket, a couple of sweatshirts or *jerseys* and a pair of long pants. There are nice restaurants, plays and events you'll want to dress for and if you're a golfer, a few courses require a shirt with a collar. If you enjoy live drama, try the Mercury Theatre in Auckland or the Downstage Theatre in Wellington.

There are also good amateur productions in smaller towns. Check in the *Tourist Information Center* or a local paper. And there's music everywhere, from Rave Concerts to the National Symphony Orchestra. Smaller towns have *Country Western Clubs, Return Service Association's (RSAs),* and other private clubs with live entertainment. And of course there's professional entertainment in *pubs* and restaurants.

You'll be cruising the supermarket aisles in confusion the first time you stock up your *movan*. Pack and Save is a discount supermarket, but bring your own bags. We carry an old backpack and string bag. You're not going very far, just out the door and into the lot or around the corner to your *movan*.

The bakery section has *crumpets, scones, pikelets* and *pavlova* — the national dessert, a concoction of stale meringue, strawberries and passion fruit. Since I don't care for meringue or passion fruit, my first and last taste left me a very poor judge of *pavlova*. *Dry biscuits* are crackers, *sweet biscuits* are cookies and *wine biscuits* don't taste like wine.

New Zealand bakeries, including those in supermarkets, have good bread. With prepackaged bread, buy a *toaster loaf* unless you want skinny little slices. These skinny little slices are often used for skinny little sandwiches. Be prepared for a surprise when you order a sandwich. A toasted sandwich might be a skinny little grilled sandwich with tomato or *marmite* filling, or a hamburger with a sunnyside up egg topping the pile.

Supermarket napkins are usually hidden away from the other paper products. Don't ask for a napkin either or you'll be directed to the *nappies*. You want the *serviettes*.

What to bring home? Fairydown sportswear. Pottery and wood carvings if you can spare a carry-on bag. Woolen products. For the best prices on sheepskins, visit the Sheepskin Tannery in Napier (NI). I had a fluffy six skin bed throw mailed home and waiting on my doorstep for almost the same price as a New Zealand haul-your-own purchase.

If it's a light item, have the sales clerk check the price difference, *GST* vs shipping. Small towns have artist co-ops with handicrafts and hand-knitted products and interesting secondhand stores. I've never been clear on the difference between antiques and junk. If you like old things, poke around. It's probably hard to leave New Zealand without at least one bargain.

Buy a prepaid mobile phone. Saves money on calls back home. We bought a *Gold Prepaid Mobile* from The Ware-house because the price was right at the time. A free phone with the purchase of a 100 $NZ phone card. It's user friendly and works fine. *Vodaphone* and *Gold Mobile* are the two main players. Check around for the best price. Just ask if there are restrictions on how often you have to use it. Our first phone had to be used at least once every six months. There are no restrictions on our *Gold Mobile*. Prepaid phone cards for *phone box* phones are also available. Rates are cheaper than credit card rates charged to your land line.

Warning: Don't bring hard luggage. Use boxes, duffle bags, soft luggage. Anything that folds flat under your mattress.
Don't forget those meds.
Don't ask for a baby diaper to wipe your face.

9

WAVE AT THE WINGS

If you're serious about spending winters in New Zealand, check out the NZMCA— The Association of Self Propelled Caravans. Founded in 1956, it has more than 23,000 members. For 50 $NZ you will become a member and receive the *Members Handbook with Travel Directory.* Subscription to the *Motor Caravanner* is separate. Subscription closes on August 31, so fees, which include your joining fee, are on a sliding scale depending on the time of year you join. Fees can be paid by Visa or Mastercard.

You're a member now. You'll receive *WINGS* with your member number for your *movan.* Fly them high and proud on your *windscreen,* and wave at the passing *WINGS.* This is your secret sign that singles you out from the rental vans.

Check your new Travel Directory when you reach a new area for:

> Dump Stations
> *Park over Properties (POPs)*

District Council Bylaws on overnight parking
Low cost or free parking
Member discount camps
Department of Conservation Camps (DOCs)
Auckland Regional Council Camps
Launderettes
Points of Interest

In your *Members Handbook,* you will find NZMCA approved *valuers,* Registered Electrical Inspectors and members who can help you obtain your self-containment certificate.

Feeding ducks at Club Friendly Trout Stream Park. Red wings are over the cab

Your *Member Handbook* has a membership list. Sneak up and eye the membership number on the *movan* parked nearby, then run back and thumb through the book to remember the name of that couple you met last month at the *EBOP Rally. Kiwi movans* are named like sailboats, "Lazy Bones," " Where Next," " See Ya." "That's 'Moochin Along.' Remember, it was parked under the bridge with us at Te Aroha."

NZMCA has two miscellaneous publications: *Codes of Construction and Recreational Vehicles Handy Hints. Handy Hints* is a good publication to have if you're planning to have a *movan* custom-built. *Handy Hints* covers:

Planning a *Movan*
Plumbing & Bathrooms
LPG for Domestic Use
Chassis & Running Gear
Movan Electrical Systems
Movan Interior
The Power Train

Study the ads in the *Motor Caravanner* for a good idea of what's available for New Zealand *movaners*. You'll find ads for "Raising the Roof on a 6-7 metre Nissan Civilian". Class A motorhomes, awnings, *motorcaravan* builders and dealers are listed as well as a classified section for privately owned vehicles — a good way to find your price range.

The Motor Caravanner is a well written publication. Besides the "Cook's Page," it carries articles about *movaning* and the latest legislation, members' input and reports from specialists on the working components of your van, such as Barry Bartlett's (#10744) *LPG* Report. "From the Press" carries reprints on *movaning* from New Zealand newspapers. You'll find announcements for special events such as the *Classic Fighters in Marlboro* — sign up and park your *movan* next to the airfield while you attend the air show with other members. *Kiwis* like their WWII vintage planes. I like the Russian Yaks that show up at most airshows.

The November 2002 Issue had articles on "Places of Interest. Wellington City Centre." "Buying a Portable Generator. What Size Do I need?" "Northern Queensland (Australia) and Outback Safari *2002*." "Land Transport Matters." "Battery Revitaliser. Now in 1-3 Dose Pack." "North to Alaska 2002."

I slipped Australia in on you, so it's a good time to meander back and mention Australia. Australia has a sister organization, *Caravan and Motorhome Club of Australia (CMCA)*, similar to NZMCA. Some *Kiwis* ship their vans to the southwest coast of Australia, then fly up and winter like Idaho snowbirds in Arizona. The shipping point of choice seems to be out of Tauranga, a mid-sized town on the Bay of Plenty, about three hours southeast of Auckland.

Before shipping, *Kiwis* remove anything of value, or secure the rear section (we found the marks in our *movan* where a panel had been screwed in to block rear access from the cab). Three days later, after a mandatory Australian steam cleaning, they hop in for an Australian circumnavigation, counterclockwise. They say, to go with the prevailing wind.

If they want to spend more than one season in Australia, there's a large popular storage facility on the southwest coast. Australia/New Zealand weather is as different as Idaho and Florida. You'll get pretty hot and wet in parts of Australia in their summer. If you're interested, talk to *Kiwis* at rallies, contact them through *The Motorcaravanner* or contact *CMCA* directly. When you put your *New* Zealand *movan* up for sale, it has to be returned to New Zealand. You can't sell it in Australia.

Three *Interislander* ferries link the North and South Island. These are ocean going vessels that zip through the Cook Strait from Wellington to Picton in three hours. Off season discounts are available to NZMCA members — rates jump beyond 3.5 metres.

Don't take this passage for granted. If you pull up unannounced in a *movan*, you'll be left cooling your heels in the middle of a Wellington freight shipping yard. Holiday season for *Kiwis* is about a month — from before Christmas till about January 20th when school resumes. During the whole month tourists bang around, but most *Kiwi* families stay close to home until after *Boxing Day*.

Part of the *Tranzrail Transportation* system, these roll-on, roll-off ferries carry commercial trucks, autos and passengers as well as small boats and *movans*. There are several departures a day, occasionally cancelled during bad weather. Those *Roaring Forties* can cause a pretty rough passage at times. Our first passage, a December passage (I can only guess how bad it gets in their winter) I couldn't even get out on the upper deck without getting soaked to see the scenery that wasn't there anyway.

Cheaper rates, if you're not already booked at a discount rate, are available if you leave at 1:30AM. This really isn't as bad as it sounds. We've booked a 6:30AM passage and slept in Tranz Rail's parking lot. There is parking space *movaners* use behind the main parking lot, not next to the railroad switching yards where we spent our first noisy night. Just pull in with the other *movaners* if you have a middle of the night or early morning passage. *Motorcamps* are not nearby. Besides, you don't want to wake everybody in camp up when you bang around getting those last minute items piled in the *boot* and fire up that diesel engine, or lose your way in an unfamiliar city and miss your passage.

After your *movan's* loaded, walk upstairs to the restaurant, lounge or bar or move out on the deck if the weather's nice and enjoy your trip.

If you're returning to the North Island, book a round trip. Figure how long you'll be in the South Island — at least a month — and make sure you're back up at Picton for the return passage on the day you're scheduled to depart. If not, expect a BIG fare hike. Passage is *dear* so it's worth your while to check out the discounts.

We like the 6:30 AM passage because we can pass through the Queen Charlotte Sound into the South Island in early morning. Keep your eye to the starboard. The Queen Charlotte Track snakes 67 km around the coves and inlets and over the ridges from Ship Cove to Anakiwa.

When you reach Picton, you'll probably want to catch up on the sleep you missed the night before. The small town of Picton is traveler-friendly with public showers near the ferry terminal. There are inexpensive *motorcamps* with a *Club Friendly Camp* in town and another around the east overlooking the Picton harbor.

When the leaves skid off your *windscreen* in late March, you'll know it's time to head home. NZMCA has a member-supervised storage/stop over facility in Paeroa, about two hours south of Auckland. You can store your *movan* either inside or out. Line up someone who'll fire it up once in a while — *movans* are kind of like old husbands. Fire them up and run them around the block every once in a while to keep the moving parts moving. We've checked out the NZMCA facility and stayed overnight, but store our *movan* at VanCo, about thirty minutes from the Auckland Airport. Robert Baile, the owner, has it ready for the road when we arrive so we're out of there in a day or two.

Join NZMCA even if you're still unsure if you're ready for that big step. Dig through their publications and ask their experts if you have questions. These are experienced *movaners*, not someone trying to sell their products. And — Wave at the *WINGS*!.

> **Warning**: No warnings here. You can't go wrong with NZMCA.

10

FREEDOM AND
LOW COST CAMPING

You didn't come to *Godzone* to stay in a *motorcamp*. You'll want a *motorcamp* occasionally to soak in a spa, get a good shower, find the bottom of the laundry bag or just hide out for a couple of days if the weather's bad. The rest of the time you'll be seeking scenery on the back roads. Pull out those *AA District Maps* and your *Travel Directory* and let's browse.

Your *Travel Directory* is divided into areas — seventeen in the North Island and eight in the South Island. Flip to the area where you hope to settle for a night or two and find a listing under Low Cost or Free Parking along the road you're traveling and mark it on the map — and the road before it — or you'll pass it on the fly. In the Rotorua area, famous for its thermal activity and *Maori* cultural exhibits, you'll find listed:

<u>Lake Maraetai</u>: Mangakino Recreation Reserve, beside Mangakino. Boat ramps & public T.

<u>Butchers Pool</u>: Off Broadland Rd, the back road between Taupo and Reporoa halfway down hill

immediately S of Reporoa. Turn E into very narrow road, over a cattle stop, along tall tree line (looks like a farm track) large timbered hot pool, some parking. No facilities.

Lake Maraetai is well marked on the map, you'll find several *movans* and campers boating or fishing, and a toilet. At Butchers Pool, you'll probably spend the evening alone or with two or three other *movaners* soaking in the hot springs.

When we're in the Taranaki area (where they filmed *The Last Samurai*) we stay at:

<u>Hawera</u>: Te Ngutu-O-Te Manu Historic Reserve near Kapuni Natural Gas Plant. W T El Pts (Water, toilet, electricity) Moderate Charges. Hawera is a *reserve* in the middle of farm country. Stop at the house near the entrance. The kids will help you find *Mum,* then park where you want. Pay 1 $NZ if you want electricity.
Sometimes one or two other NZMCA *movans* pull in. Usually we're alone. Like most *reserves*, it's a large grass area surrounded by *bush*. In the morning, take a walk along the *bush* path and visit the fantails. They'll flick past your nose, sit on the branch next to you and fan out their tail.

The nearby Tawhiti Museum in a converted cheese factory focuses on colonial and *Maori* history of South Taranaki. All displays including the life-size figures cast from real people are designed and built at the factory. I enjoy the scale model diorama of the musket wars. Nigel Ogle started this privately owned museum as a hobby. He wanted his displays three dimensional and not just old dusty junk. This certainly is one museum worth visiting. <u>www.tawhitimuseum.co.nz</u>.

When we *freedom camp*, we're often on *reserves*, but we've stayed at <u>Ramui Buses</u> in the *EBOP* area. Ramui Buses, behind the BP in Opotiki, a storage facility for buses, is just fine after we've passed through the mountains and just want a place to stay overnight before heading down the coast. In Hawks Bay area, near the tennis courts at the <u>Tikokino Sports Complex,</u> they leave the *loos* open for us. In the morning we walk all two blocks of the town checking out the gardens before we leave for the Onga Onga golf course.

The Army Museum in Waiouru South of Lake Taupo (NI) is so impressive, we stop every year in the freedom park behind the museum. Their lifelike displays begin with *Gate Pa*, an 1864 battle where two hundred fifty *Maori* defeated almost two thousand British troops. In 1915, New Zealand sent eight and a half thousand men to fight on the cliffs and in the trenches of Gallipoli. Around seven and a half thousand were killed. Almost every New Zealand family suffered a loss at Gallipoli, I was told. Displays carry you through Korea and Vietnam.

<u>Quinney's Bush</u> near Nelson (SI) was started by Ray Quinney in 1961 to raise funds for a new vicarage at Tapawera. Back then, it had a *long-drop*. The *long-drop* is long gone, but it's still a back-to-basics family camp that doesn't tolerate "noisy parties, loud music or drunken behavior" so behave yourself. If you want a hot shower, drop some chips in the burner and wait a while. Really a nice place to stay. I just prefer my own shower.

Rural golf courses are ideal. Occasionally a caretaker lives nearby, but usually everybody goes home and we have the whole course to ourselves. When we play golf, we ask permission to stay and have always been welcome. The manager asks if we need the *facilities* open all night.

Quinney's Bush — add some chips and stoke up the burner for a hot shower

The women's *facilities* have fancy flowers, fancy towels and good smelling shampoo and bath products. The women's *facilities* only. Dave says it's always 'bring your own soap and no flowers' on his side.

Some golf courses are listed in the *POPS*. Whangarei Golf Club (NI) has *facilities* available during club hours. There is a five night maximum stay. If you're a golfer, watch that overhanging tree on the 6th tee. It's easy to tee off and end up with the ball fifty yards behind you. A few golf courses offer electrical points for a small fee. I would guess from asking around that the courses listed in the *Travel Directory* have NZMCA members.

If you're a golfer, buy the New Zealand Golf Guide. Thirty $NZ. You'll have to ask at the proshop. They'll probably be tucked under the counter. This guide lists New Zealand courses and offers discounts to Golf Guide holders. It has information on the courses and directions to find them. Dave believes in a no nonsense approach to golf — head for the pin. I take the scenic route. That's how I found the hedgehog and the strange looking flowers. We both enjoy the Rangatira Golf Club north of Hunterville (NI). Golf Guide holders 10 $NZ. Rangatira is played on three levels. Tee off on the top level, play along the Rangitikei River, then ride the cable car back to the clubhouse from the 18th green.

Park Over Properties (POPs) are similar yet different. If you're bouncing down the road and see the *WINGS* on a mailbox, that's a *POP*. *POP* stops are listed in the *Travel Directory*. Often homes of members — look for the (m) in the listing — a *POP* can be anything from a farm on the beach to a parking spot in someone's back yard. At

Ngongotaha (NI), we swing back the gate, pull in the back yard and park on the lawn of a small motel on Lake Rotorua. There is a small charge if we want to use the spa. We show up every year and they dig potatoes for our dinner and tell us to pick what we want from the fruit trees.

You'll want to spend time around Lake Rotorua. It's a tourist area with tourist prices. Not far from the *POP* is Waiteti Trout Stream Holiday Park — *Club Friendly* after January. To reach the *POP* and Trout Stream Holiday Park, you pass the Agrodome with its live sheep shows. Fun. Sheep dogs bring in nineteen breeds of champion rams. And the rams stand on the stage and behave while you watch a shearing display and sheep dog trials. Lots more going on, so check out the Agrodome.

There are two Top Ten Holiday Parks near Rotorua. Holden Bay Holiday Park is close to the Rotorua airport. You'll have low flying commercial planes buzzing over your head. Blue Lake Holiday Park is up in the mountains about five minutes out of town. Right on the lake, it's quiet and beautiful. Beyond Blue Lake and Green Lake is the buried village. In 1848 Te Wairoa village was established by a Christian missionary. It later became popular as tourists came to visit the eighth wonder of the world, the Pink and White Terraces. In 1886, Mt. Tarawere erupted destroying the terraces and burying Te Wairoa. Parts of the village are excavated including the blacksmith shop and Tohungo's *Whare,* the house of the *Maori* high priest who predicted the destruction. He remained buried for one hundred hours but died several days later. The buried Village is uncrowded and a good place to wander and appreciate the power of nature.

Some *POP*s are service clubs such as the <u>Bullers Workingmen's Club</u> in Buller (SI). W.T. Shower (water, toilet, shower) Thurs-Sunday–donation. Meals available. Most service clubs have a bar and restaurant.

At the Paeroa *POP* — you've heard that one before, the home of Paeroa Water and also the NZMCA storage facility — they have parking spaces with power points next to the public *loos* in the middle of town. Leave a donation to cover electricity in the Information Center — just drop it in the *honesty box*.

Paeroa hosts the motorcycle race finals in February. They close off the streets, pile straw and sacks of plastic pop bottles around the hard spots, and tear around town. Best to bring your ear plugs. The cycles zip around the corner — usually. Side cars bang by, driver in front, feet-dragging passenger in back, trying to manuever around the turns. When the races are in town *movans* move to the town *reserve*. Motorcycles often miss the turn at the *POP* and you don't want a cycle in your bed. If you're uncomfortable by yourself, stay in a *POP* — there'll always be someone around.

Try the *Club Friendly Camps*. Seven $NZ per van off-season, Feb 7th-Dec 7th. Some offer low rates all year. Rates are listed in *The Motorcaravanner and Handbook*. Don't argue with the manager trying to get a special rate in their busy season. They have a very short tourist season to pay their year-round bills. And don't abuse your discount privilege by telling the visitors in the adjacent site you're paying less.

At <u>Huntley Motor Camp</u> (NI), pull in by the lake. Just make sure you have bread for the ducks and a snack for the camp *moggy*. At Hastings (NI) stay at the *Club Friendly* <u>Raceview Motel and Holiday Park</u> and watch the *gallops* from your lawn chair. <u>Cambridge Motor Park</u>, though not listed as a *Club Friendly Camp,* is quiet, very nice and charges 10 $NZ (2 people with power) all year. Rates in most *motorcamps* are based on number of people per van.

You'll want to stay in Cambridge if you're going to the Mystery Creek Car Show. Dave's a car junky. There were so many antique cars at Mystery Creek — many he'd never seen before — he wore out in the afternoon and we never did get to see them all. *Kiwis* don't haul their old cars to shows, either. They drive them. You'll see convoys of old cars, sometimes parked along the highway trying to get one of them up and chugging again.

Show your NZMCA card when checking into a *motorcamp*. It usually means some kind of a discount unless you're checking into a TOP 10, then pull out your TOP 10 or KOA card.

Department of Conservation Camps — Te Papa Atawhai (*DOC* camps) are government *reserves.* If you really want to nose back into untouched country, try a *DOC* camp. Directions, facilities and fees are listed in the *Travel Directory.* Reduced rate *DOC* passes are available to NZMCA members, however these passes are not valid at all *DOC reserves.* Application forms are in *The Motor Caravanner.* There are restrictions on maximum stay and type of vehicle. *Movans*, buses and other vehicles designed to sleep people are acceptable, but not a car. We've stayed at *DOC* camps, but never long enough to make a pass worthwhile. For further information, find a local *DOC* office, meander in and check out the maps and brochures or try www.doc.govt.nz.

White Horse Hill (SI): Adj SH 80, Mt Cook Village, follow Hooker Valley Rd for 2 km. Access (through fording) not suitable for lge veh, W.T.P.R. (Water, toilet, power, rubbish removal. Some are pack-it-in, pack-it-out) 5 $NZ pp. About 5 $US for two people.

Lake Waikaremoana rates run from 60 $NZ for a self-contained chalet to 7.50 $NZ for a tent site. Five thousand people per year visit, many to fish for brown and rainbow trout or to *tramp* the *Lake Waikaremoana Track*. The track, a 46 km three to four day *tramp* which follows the lakeshore, is part of the "Great Walks" managed by the *DOC*.

Te Paki Recreation Reserve on the tip of the North Island on the Aupouri Peninsula — that finger that pokes up toward Australia with Ninety Mile Beach on it's western side — is managed by the *Department of Lands and Survey* for recreation and the protection of the environment. It's divided into four *reserves* and is one of the largest wildlife habitats in New Zealand. Te Paki has a breeding colony for many birds and is also the home of the Green Gecko, who's just as cute as his relative on our *telly* commercials.

We stayed at Tapotupotu Bay for 6 $NZ pp, where I decided I'd *tramp* back to the Cape Reinga lighthouse early one morning. That didn't last long. Even a mountain goat would get winded on that one.

I haven't said much about the South Island. There's more people in Auckland than the whole South Island. Nelson, one of the warmest areas of New Zealand in the northwest near the Tasman Sea, is a vacation/retirement area. Christchurch on the east coast and Dunedin further down the coast are the major cities of the South Island.

Bunji jumping near Queenstown

Queenstown is the "Adventure Capitol." <u>Queenstown Top 10 Holiday Park</u> is listed as a *Members Discount Camp*, but use your Top 10 or KOA card. This *motorcamp* is within walking distance of Lake Wakatipu and downtown shops and restaurants. It's also a short walk to the Skyline Gondola which takes you to the top where you can parasail, enjoy a view of Queenstown and Lake Wakatipu and the Remarkables, ride the dry land Luge or watch "Kiwi Magic," a funny film with spectacular New Zealand scenery.

If you're hungry, enjoy the buffet while you watch the sunset. Just remember to get dinner reservations.

The rest of the South Island is pretty remote. Many *Kiwis* who tour the South Island *freedom camp* or use *POPs*. If you see a good looking spot, pull over and ask about. We did. Just make sure you're not on *Maori* tribal land. Only thing to watch for are bugs — teeny ones that wiggle through your screens even in the daytime — and noisy bull elk. You'll find elk farms in the South Island.

When I saw my first billy goat running down the road in front of us with a trail of sheep following him, I said, "Oh poor goat." A few billy goats later, I found out he was a bad billy that didn't like to stay home. He's not wearing a fence, that's his wooden collar to keep him from a breakout. The farmer probably wouldn't care if he left, but the sheep tag along for the excitement.

I mentioned ferry discounts after February 7th. That's the best time to visit the South Island. Figure northern US weather, August 7th.

Wherever you spend the night, *freedom camping,* in a *POP*, or *motorcamp*, you'll find a bargain.

> **Warning:** Be there for your return trip ferry date.
>   Watch the overhanging tree on the 6th tee at Whangarei Golf Club.
>   Don't eat dinner before you ride *The Luge* in Queenstown.
>   Don't park too close to an estuary at low tide. You might wake up floating
>   Don't park next to a hippy in a teepee with a bongo drum

11

FOR THE BIRDS

I like birds, especially New Zealand birds. They seem to have a sense of humor just like the *Kiwi*s. Don't expect a Kiwi bird to wander into camp mooching food. They're nocturnal. Good sized birds, bigger than a chicken, with brown bristly feathers, dark legs and a long pointed beak they poke in the dirt in search of insects or fallen fruit.

The best place to see a Kiwi bird is in a bird sanctuary. If you're near the Waitomo Glo Worm Caves, try the Otorohanga Kiwi House. In the South Island, try the *DOC's* Mt. Bruce National Wildlife Centre. Birds are in their native environment. You walk along the paths and climb platforms in the trees. The birds are not looking for a handout or trying to impress you.

We've heard Kiwi birds call at night. At least *Kiwi*s have told us that's what we heard, and I accidentally stirred one up in his burrow during the daytime on the South Island. We'd pulled into a small parking spot on a very windy road. It was my job to stand in the road, check for traffic around the curve and get Dave out and about as quickly as possible so we didn't get rear ended.

I cut through the *bush*, was startled to see a Kiwi bird staggering around, and frantically waved "Come on" for Dave to see the Kiwi. He thought I meant, "Get with it." He pulled out into the road, I ran for the door and we charged off, probably leaving a grumbling Kiwi bird complaining about the inconsiderate tourists.

The Moreporks are also nocturnal. These small owls have a distinct call. I like to flip open the vent over our bed, watch the stars and listen to them call back and forth through the *bush*.

My favorite bird is the Fantail. About the size of a chubby sparrow with an apricot breast and white ear patch, these show-offs, often in pairs or groups, tag along through the *bush*, zip past your nose, then sit on a branch and flip open their fan tail. Tell them how pretty they are and they'll hop around so you can see the back view. It's hard not to smile with a Fantail flashing you.

Tui birds, good singers, about the size of a crow, are dark greenish black with a metalic sheen. They have a big white feathery bump on their throats and white patches on their wings. These nectar stealers often hang around the motorparks, riding a big bouncing flower.

The Kea lives in the South Island high-country forests. About the size of a hawk, this olive green parrot with orange underwing is a good-looking bird — that's a pest. Nosy and destructive, they'll mess up anything you leave lying around. The stories told about these little buggers are funny, if it's not your equipment they've destroyed.

These are all native birds. New Zealand also has a lot of *tourist over-stayers*. There's even a California Quail.

I'm not a bird expert. I picked up Geoff Moon's *Common Birds in New Zealand* and we thumb through it when we run across a new bird.

We end up at least once or twice a year at Lake Tutira, north of Napier (NI). I like to sleep near the Black Swans. Introduced from Australia in the 1860's, you'll find Black Swans on most lakes. At Lake Tutira, you can pull up next to the lake and listen to the swans toot and whistle all night.

Camping with the black swans at Lake Tutira (NI)

As I said, I know little about birds, except sparrows are moochers, so friendly they eat out of Dave's hand. But these swans must have a sentry on duty all night. Somebody's always crooning a lullaby.

A short distance away at Cape Kidnappers in Hawks Bay, there's an Australasian Gannet colony. Cape Kidnappers was named when Captain Cook and his crew of the Endeavor had an unfriendly encounter with the local *Maori's*. Today, you won't find unfriendly *Maori's,* only wing-to-wing poop and sea weed-cemented nests where up to 6500 pairs of Gannets arrive each August. Wings swept back, these golden-necked sea birds drop out of the sky and smash into the sea in search of dinner. Often mating for life, they stroke necks, preen each other and then take turns protecting the eggs with their large webbed feet. In March, the new families head north back across the Tasman Sea. You can't, and wouldn't want to pull your *movan* close to the three main nesting sites. You can walk in (at low tide), kayak or travel with a guide in a small tractor-trailer.

The Miranda Shorebird Centre, owned by the Miranda Naturalists' Trust is a volunteer non-profit organization. Located about an hour south of Auckland near the mouth of the Firth of Thames, it has three bunk rooms plus two self-contained flats. We've stayed overnight at the centre in our *movan*. Wading birds arrive down the EastAsia Australia Flyway from their breeding grounds in eastern Siberia and Alaska. Not with a cocktail and a movie in a pressurized jet, either. And you thought you were the first one to come up with the idea of a winter in New Zealand?

you like birds, why not join the Miranda Banders and get out there in the mud — actually it's done at high tide with a cannon-net. Or, help with repairs at the Centre and then head up the road to the _Miranda Holiday Park_ and soak in the mineral pool.

Even if your New Zealand trip is in the future, help them out by joining. Overseas membership is 30 $NZ. The quarterly Miranda News which members receive is well worth it. Find out what's happening along this least understood of the world's wader flyways.

If you join the Royal Forest and Bird Protection Society of New Zealand, you'll receive a beautiful full color quarterly magazine as well as the listing of Forest & Bird Lodges. Check their web site at www.forest-bird.org.nz. You'll need reservations to stay at the lodge, but we've asked and been allowed to stay the night at Tautuku (SI) in our _movan_. In the morning, we wandered down one of the walking paths. Tautuku Lodge is located on the Lenz Reserve owned by the Royal Forest and Bird Protection Society. The reserve was purchased for the benefit of the locals — the feathered variety, not visiting _movaners_.

Although bookings for the lodge or cabins are available to nonmembers, be sure to pay your way. Even if overnighting in your own _movan_, a donation is appreciated. This is another non-profit organization. In the Lenz reserve, you'll find waterfalls, beaches, forests and sea birds, including the rare yellow-eyed penguin.

Yes. I said penguins. The little Blue Penguin is common in New Zealand. At Oamaru (SI), we settled into _Oamaru Gardens Holiday Park._ Later in the evening, we sat on wooden bleachers waiting for the Blue Penguins to swim ashore in a penguin raft, climb the cliff, then mingle around nearby trying to get up the nerve to waddle across the dirt road to the squawking chicks.

Nesting holes in the cliffs and burrows are in short supply, so local school children build penguin condos from scrap lumber and check the nests daily for any orphans who need to be hand-fed. By dawn the next morning, parent penguins are out to sea searching for food and you can walk the paths among the nests. I can't think of a better way to spend a night than watching Blue Penguins deliver dinner or listening to a wild symphony of Moreporks or Black Swans. Just don't leave your hiking boots outside in Kea country.

From a glassed-in *Department of Commerce* observatory on the wind-swept Taiaroa Head near Otago (SI), you can watch the Royal Albatrosses. These elegant giants arrive each year in September, stay nearly a year building nests and raising chicks before paragliding off the windy cliffs for a year at sea circling the Antarctic.

Most bird sanctuaries do not allow dogs and cats. This won't be a problem for you. You won't be bringing a dog or a cat. New Zealand is a rabies-free country and wants to stay that way. Dogs and cats from the US are impounded for six months until they are certified "healthy." We have three cats. They stay home and guard the house.

Warning: Don't forget to save bread crumbs for those cheeky little sparrows
Hang on to your hat in Kea Country

12

LET'S GET WET

I've met other worn-out sailors turned RVers. Even three steps up and down from cabin to cockpit a hundred times a day, sooner or later starts to ache those worn-out knees and crusty joints. There are cruisers and day sailors. For lack of a better description, cruisers live aboard, poke around and anchor out or wharf-hop. Day Sailors usually like to race with the closest boat, even if that boat doesn't know it's racing, then hang around the dock or the clubhouse at the end of the day and swap rose-colored sail tales.

New Zealand, though it's the land of top mega yacht racers, is not a cruiser-friendly country. Opua, in the throat of the Bay of Islands (NI), twenty one days from Tonga, is a *hurricane hole* for an international collection of yachts. There is a small store with good ice cream where you cue up for the mini-auto ferry to Russel and not much else. Although the Northland and Far North have an occasional hurricane, Opua is tucked in tight.

Like snorkeling or scuba diving? Charter a boat to the

nearby Poor Knights for some of the best snorkeling and diving in the world. Further down the east coast is Whangarei, where you might find a slip at the crowded boat basin. If not, you anchor out. And further on down is Auckland, the City of Sails.

You can also get in at Tauranga, Wellington, Picton or Christchurch. But where do you go from there? Remember, you're straddling the *Roaring Forties*. A circumnavigation of the island is possible with a little good weather and a lot of luck, but the west coast is so shallow, it's pretty hard to get in anywhere. Remember the movie *The Piano*? It was filmed on the east coast of the North Island.

If you want to cruise, rent a yacht at Opua, hop in and tour the Bay of Islands. The weather's warm, the water's warm and the fishing's hot. Take it out yourself or hire a skipper and sit back and enjoy a beer while you burn. New Zealand is close to that hole in the ozone we've been watching for years. You can turn to toast in a hurry even on a cool cloudy day. So slip, slap, slop as the *Kiwi* signs remind you. Slip on a shirt, slap on a hat, and slop on the suntan lotion.

If you're a fisherman, you'll want to get out in a boat at least once on the ocean or on one of the large lakes. Charter with a skipper in the Bay of Islands if you're looking for a swordfish, shark or tuna. Or just talk it up with a *Kiwi* at a rally if you want to get out for some inland fishing. Remember that free drink I bragged about getting for a secondhand New Zealand Herald? That *Kiwi* was a retired fishing guide on Lake Taupo. He offered a lakeside *POP* in his backyard and a day on Lake Taupo, where world record brown trout hang out.

New Zealand Lakes are famous for brown and rainbow trout. January to March are good months to visit the South Island east coast if you're a salmon fisherman. Pick up a *New Zealand Fishing News* at a bookstore or the *post shop* or contact www.fishing.net.nz. Each local region has its own fishing rules. *Fish and Game New Zealand*, www.fishand-game.org.nz, can provide copies of regulations and seasons or visit a local *DOC* office.

At least take the Cream Boat trip in the Bay of Islands, the Mail Boat in Marlboro Sound and the trip to White Island. In Taranaki (NI), ride up the river on the restored paddlesteamer Waimarie. Help shovel coal or sit back while the guides point out local points of interest along the banks — the church with the tower that *looks* crooked or the *Maori* burial site from the musket war.

Waiting for the mail in Marlboro Sound (SI)

With so much water around, you can hop on a boat and enjoy the scenery almost anywhere. Rafting or kayaking your cup of tea? How about three to five days gliding or bouncing down a river checking out the unspoiled locations? Two skinny islands jammed with unspoiled rivers makes it easy to get into the wilderness in a hurry. Don't try rafting or kayaking without an experienced guide. Weather changes quickly on those two skinny islands. A cloudburst can rapidly change a Grade 3 river into a Grade 5. Besides, the guide will pack your gear, fix your meals and set up camp along the beach or bank each night. The New Zealand *Professional Rafting Association,* www.nzrafting.co.nz, can float you in the right direction.

Pick your first river carefully. The Mighty Motu (NI) can munch your hinney and spit it out along the bank. You'll get your thrills and chills — if you get dumped. But, if something goes wrong, you're a long way from a soft bed, a nice warm lemonade or a paramedic. The Wanganui River is ideal for beginners. You'll float along in the wilderness without white water knuckles, then camp each night at a maintained hut or camp. High water levels for (NI) rivers — September to December. Low levels — January to March.

If you're interested in a few days off in the *bush* — remember nothing bad is going to bite you — send for the *New Zealand Canoeing Association's* guide book to fifteen hundred rivers, each graded with bad parts highlighted. www.rivers.org.nz.

And don't forget the jet boats in Queenstown (SI) and Taupo (NI). Jump in, tighten your helmet and hang on.

Your trip to New Zealand won't be complete unless you get wet, one way or the other.

> **Warning**: Slip, slap, slop — or sizzle
>   Don't wander off in the bush. It's easy to get lost

13

RIDE THE RAILS —
OR HOP ON THE BUS

Like trains? Me, too. My father, a railroad engineer, sang *The Wreck of the Old 97* when he cooked dinner. With my railroad pass, I disappeared on Fridays, rode the "Milk Train" which was slower than the slow boat to China, and managed to wake up as we pulled into Dunsmuir Monday morning in time to climb the hill for my first period high school class. That clickity clack got me at an early age. Those were the days when passenger trains ran on time.

New Zealand trains are still fun. *Tranzrail* runs from Auckland to Invercargill on the tip of the South Island with spur lines to Tauranga, Rotorua and Napier in the North Island.

The narrow-guage Tranz Alpine Express charges from Christchurch (SI) across the Canterbury Plains. At Springfield, you can bang around in an open observation car in the rear taking pictures as the Tranz Alpine snakes through nineteen tunnels and across river gorges on high spindly viaducts. At Arthur's Pass you can hop off with the *trampers* for a quick *tiki tour* of the station — it will probably be drizzling — before heading for the Otira Tunnel.

When it opened in 1923, Otira tunnel was the seventh longest in the world. Passing through the tunnel, the observation car is closed and fresh air is blown in for the diesel engines. Rocks rush past your nose in the dark, then you pop out of your hole like the white rabbit into the soft damp west coast rain forest.

Another brief stop at glacial Lake Brunner, where more passengers pile out, then the Tranz Alpine drops down the Arnold and Grey River to Greymouth on the Tasman Sea. Have lunch at Greymouth and be back to Christchurch by early evening. Or, spend the night and come back the next day.

If it sounds like fun, it is. Ask for Tranz Rail's *Great Train Escapes* and *Trains Planes and Ferries* as well as *Train Fares and Timetables*. Look for special fares including Day Excursion, Senior Saver and Super Saver Fares — 50% off at off-peak times. Check www.Tranz-scenic.co.nz for long-distance passenger trains in New Zealand.

You'll find the Kingston Flyer in the *Tranz Scenic* brochures. We park our *movan* at Kingston (SI) and get up early — you won't sleep with the steam locomotive puffing by your bed. See the NZMCA Handbook — it's listed under free parking. Enjoy the hour and a half round trip excursion in a restored 1898 "Birdcage" compartment carriage. They can even arrange a "Hold-up" of the train if you're traveling with a grouchy companion.

The Goldfields Railway diesel or steam locomotives run

from Waihi to Waikino (NI) daily. Locomotive *drivers* are volunteers. At Waihi — you're in gold country again — take the PR tour of the working Martha Mine. I'm not too sure how much of this one to believe. You're given a tour of the operation, including a tailings and waste disposal pond where "a wide variety of bird species are frequent visitors." There weren't any feathered visitors the day we were there.

When you reach Waikino, pick up a walking map in the

The Kingston Flyer warming up for the day

train station and check out the New Zealand railroad books if you're a railroad buff. Then, cross under the road and spend a few hours in the old battery and check out the abandoned rail tunnels. The battery is being restored. It's a good place for a picnic or some unusual photo shots.

In the Coromandel (NI), zig zag on the Possum three kms up a steep grade, through tree ferns and tunnels. You'll pass recycled wine bottle retaining walls sparkling in the sun and a smiling ceramic dragon, then cross bridges and a double-deck viaduct to a spectacular view across the Firth of Thames.

This fifteen inch narrow gauge was built by Barry Bickle, a man with a shovel and a strong back, to carry clay and firewood to the potteries at the base of the mountain. Barry is slowly replanting his man-made native hillside, damaged by loggers and California gold diggers. His project survives mainly on donations. "I've applied for grants, but nobody's going to give a grant to a loud-mouth eccentric," he says.

A working gold stamper battery is nearby, and also Waterworld, a two acre park with water driven gadgets, machines and sculptures, built by another self-proclaimed eccentric.

Buses are another way to get around. The stations are clean, convenient and the buses run on time. Even with a *movan*, we rent cars and ride buses.

Inter City Coachlines, can take you just about any place you want to go. Ask for their *National Timetable*. It has fares and schedules including private operators. You'll find the 3-in- One travel pass for *Inter City Coachlines, Newmans Coachlines*, the *Tranz Scenic* rail services and the *Interislander* ferry. The 3-in-One pass allows one flight with Air New Zealand or Ansett New Zealand as part of the pass. Ask for coach pass information if you're interested in a specific area. www.intercitycoach.co.nz. Guided tours are available — different adventures for different age groups. *Flying Kiwi Wilderness Expeditions* and *Magic Traveler* bus tours are geared to a younger, more energetic group. www.flyingkiwi.co.nz. www.magicbus.co.nz.

When we see a *Magic Bus* coming out of a *metal* road, we check to see what we missed. They tend to find unique out-of-the-way spots for their clients.

The shuttle bus between Auckland Airport and downtown Auckland is a snap, too.

I promised in the beginning this wasn't a travel guide, but I've mentioned nearby places, "Oh, by the way, if you're there, see . . ." That's the best way to travel. With a *movan* if you find something that interests you, find a place to *freedom park* or a *motorcamp* and do it the next day. The guided tour won't take off while you're in the *loo*.

I haven't mentioned fares either. Bus and train fares can be as changeable as the New Zealand weather. Figure out when and where you're going and how long you'll be there, then find the fare.

Warning: Don't miss the Tranz Alpine, and bring
plenty of film
Don't fall off the Possom

14

TRAMPING THE TRACKS

The first time we were invited to go *tramping*, I remembered my early days — lunch in a bandana draped from a stick over my shoulder, playing hobo for a day. Now I have a *movan* and just dig in the cupboard if I want a dry peanut butter sandwich. *Kiwis* don't disappear into the bush to enjoy a picnic. They disappear for days — *tramping*. They even join tramping clubs. I warned you not to wander off into the bush, but *tramping* is different. New Zealand has well marked *tracks* with camps and huts along the way.

We *tramp* and *trek*, but not for long. I like my own bed and don't want to carry more than my lunch. One of the nicest early morning *tramps* is around Lake Matheson (SI). It's easy walking with bridges across the rough spots. On a calm morning you can see Mt. Tasman and Mt Cook reflected in the lake water. Every small town information center offers free maps of trails and *tracks* in their area. The more popular *tracks are* in the Jasons Route Planners

For a three to five day adventure, you'll need good

quality equipment and a *National Parks* or *Forest Service* map. Most *National Parks* have *Department of Lands and Surveys rangers* who have radio contact with the outside world. In *State Forest Parks*, you're pretty much on your own. *Forest Service* huts — first come, first serve — have toilets, running water and firewood for a small charge. *National parks, forest parks, marine reserves* and *reserves* are managed by the *Department of Conservation–Te Papa Atawhai (DOC)*.

For an extended *trek*, consider a guide. You pay more and carry less — those backpacks get heavy after the first mile. When you stop for the day, let someone else set up camp and fix dinner. Pick your first *trek* carefully. You don't want to be so exhausted you can't enjoy the view.

Kiwi friends *tramped* the Milford Track (SI) for her 60th birthday. He was a little older. This popular track is much the same as ninety years ago when it was discovered as an overland access to Milford Sound. Called one the best walks in the world, the *track* wanders through the rain forest, around streams, past waterfalls and over swinging bridges for fifty kms. I asked her if it was hard. "Oh, no. It's pretty flat." You must be booked in advance with the Chief Ranger in Fiordland whether you go with a guide or *freedom walk*.

The fifty km, three to four day *track* around the edge of Lake Waikaremoana (NI) is a little more difficult, but a good trail for beginners. That's the lake with the *motorcamp* and furnished chalets I talked about before.

I want to try the Abel Tasman National Park Coastal Track. Four days, golden sand beaches and easy walking through the native bush, I'm told. And the best part, if you

The end of the track at Milford Sound

don't want to spend the night on a bunk in a hut, a boat will bring you back for a hot shower and soft bed in your motel room or *movan* each night.

The Tongariro National Park Track circles three mountains for ten days, mostly uphill.

On the Copeland Pass across the Southern Alps in Mt. Cook National Park, you'll find heights and bad weather, and you'll need crampons to get across the ice. If you're still interested, find a guide and don't blame me for your blisters. Try these two organizations to get you started: *New Zealand Alpine Club*, www.nzalpine.org.nz and *Federated Mountain Clubs of New Zealand*, www.fmc.org.nz.

If you want to *tramp* and don't have a lot of experience, start with the Milford Track, the Routeburn Track, the Abel Tasman National Park Walk or Lake Waikaremoana and then move on up to Mt. Tongariro. NZMCA's *Van Trampers* can help you get started. See the next chapter.

DOC brochures classify *tracks* as: Path, well-formed track suitable for the average family. Walking track, well-defined track suitable for people of good average physical fitness. Tramping track, a less well-defined trail with often steep gradients. Route, lightly marked route for use only by well-equipped, experienced trampers. Stop into a local *DOC* office for a map, hut information or details on individual walks. Or contact www.doc.gov.nz.

On most *tramps* you'll cover about five miles a day. And you will get wet — remember *Godzone's* unpredictable weather. Bring some comfortable well-worn boots and your old backpack. You don't want to find that your fancy new pack pulls on your shoulders or pokes your hip.

Walkways are well marked and graded. Some run through private farmland. If you're a Nervous Nelly in the *wop wops*, walk across farmland. Just watch out for those Jersey bulls — they have bad reputations. Contact the *New Zealand Walkway Commission*. They'll head you in the right direction.

Farm Parks are coastal lands set aside to protect native vegetation, historic sites and scenic areas, including farmland. Farmed by the *Department of Land and Survey* you can wander through and watch them shear and dip sheep or anything else happening on a working farm, and maybe more than you care to see. Farm life can get a little bloody at times. Te Paki Farm Park is near Cape Reinga (NI). Marlboro Titirangi Farm Park is in the Marlboro Sounds near Picton (SI)

There's more than one way to get out to your own private holiday escape. Jet boats will transport you up the river and float plane pilots will drop you on a remote beach with supplies and pick you up a few days later. Bring your own boots and backpacks, but camping supplies can be purchased or rented. If you're an outdoor enthusiast, one browse through a sporting goods supply store and you'll be calculating just how much you can stuff in your suitcase — or cardboard boxes and duffel bags if you traveled smart. You'll find top quality equipment at reasonable prices.

If you plan *tramping*, even a daily jaunt around town picking up supplies or down to the beach to surf fish or poke for shells, you'll soon work out those cricks in your joints and backside from too much time in the office or that well worn recliner next to the TV zapper.

Warning: Watch those little biting buggers. Carry insect repellant.
Cut your toenails. You'll have to walk downhill once in a while.

You might have noticed I didn't mention cycling. Cycling is so popular there's even an assembly station at the Auckland Airport. Pack it in, put it together and you're out of there. We've seen families cycling with tents and whatever strapped on or hauled behind, pumping <u>very</u> slowly up a steep grade in the pouring rain or blistering sun. *Kiwis* are wild drivers, you're driving on the wrong side of the road, and the roads are windy and narrow with tight shoulders, if any at all. If you want to spend your remaining time in New Zealand in a well-tended graveyard, bring a bicycle.

15

HAVE A RALLY GOOD TIME

To meet some really good folks, join a NZMCA rally. Rallies, rendevous, get togethers — whatever we call them — we've been getting together to trade, meet new people and party since our club carrying days. The Indians and mountain men threw some pretty impressive rallies in our early western frontier days. The *Kiwis* carry on the tradition — with a lot less drinking and fighting.

The NZMCA is divided into twenty-five Area Membership Clubs, seventeen in the North Island, eight in the South Island. Check the Future Rallies section of *The Motor Caravanner* and find one nearby.

We've been to *Counties'* Christmas Rally with one hundred twenty-eight *movans* and a *Northland* rally with six *movans*. It's possible to find something going on every weekend.

Last year we met "Peter the Pom," a *Freewheeler* from England. He didn't like England's winters, bought a small *movan* and traveled around the North Island, checking out the local dance clubs when he wasn't attending a rally. Peter's a good dancer. Most single men don't seem to realize that's a secret to success with women.

Small fees are collected by the Rally Marshal to cover expenses or donations to a local organization. A rally can turn up anywhere — a school, the *A & P Showgrounds,* a boy's camp or a private club — almost anyplace several *movans* will fit. It's usually a "pack it in, pack it out policy." If *facilities* are available, they'll be mentioned in the rally announcement. We always dump our tanks and top off our water, just in case.

Once there, getting around to local attractions is not a problem. Members look out for each other. If you need a ride and don't want to move your *movan,* the Rally Marshals usually have transportation arranged. Just squeeze in with everybody else and enjoy the local sights, and many you'd never get a chance to see if you traveled on your own. It's BYOC (bring your own chair) for morning tea, happy hour and evening entertainment. If you're a musician, bring your instrument. You'll be invited to join in.

Many rallies have local musicians — good local musicians — for evening entertainment. And *Kiwis* like to dance. They're not shy, either. They get out there and get their exercise. A favorite is *Ghost Riders in the Sky.* They line up on two sides then take turns galloping down the aisle whacking their *bums* to keep the make-believe ponies on the move while swinging their make-believe lariats over their heads.

Each area has a different rally style. We've toured private gardens, played golf, spent a Country Western weekend and watched an air show.

In Manawhenua (NI) last year, we parked in the paddy on a 550 acre working dairy farm. We toured the farm on the owner's tractor trailer and watched the cows come home to the milking barn, in a nice quiet orderly line. They stepped one by one onto the turntable and rode their merry-go-round to the other end then stepped off with a smile on their face. Did you know dairy cows like flowers and soft music in their milking barn?

Lining up for a rally at Lake Rotoma Boys Brigade Camp

In the evenings, we sat on hay bales around the perimeter of the calving barn and enjoyed the singing and dancing. A little hard to shuffle around on a packed dirt floor, but it can be done. We always try to make at least one *EBOP* (Eastern Bay of Plenty) rally each year just because the people are so friendly. We picked up a hunk of driftwood a few years ago at one of their rallies that looked like a tiki god. He banged around in our *loo* for three months then stood guard outside the *movan* during the night. We got so attached to Uga Uga, we packed him in a spare sail bag and brought him home to guard our front yard. Uga Uga bounced off the American Airline turnstile that trip unharmed. Dave's luggage disappeared and hasn't been seen since.

In late March, we attend the Annual Pumpkin Rally at Bulmer's Landing (NI), listed in NZMCA's free and low cost parking. It's BYO pumpkin, plastic bottles and candles to enter the contest. Do a little fishing when you finish carving your pumpkin. In New Plymouth (NI) enjoy the Homebrew and Pickles Rally — just don't get pickled.

Special Interest Groups join regular rallies and hold their own.

Heavyweights (the Big Boys) pick spots high, wide and solid for their rallies.

Good News Vanners usually find a Christian Centre.

Van Trampers show up at *DOC* camps or *Club Friendly Campgrounds* where you might have to squeeze in. Participation is sometimes restricted due to space limitations. *Trampers* are responsible for their own gear, food and hut passes. Check with the Rally Marshal in advance and read their "track tips." Some *tracks* require advance booking. There's a little note in the 2003 *Van Tramper Programmer* — "Participation in all trips is at your own risk."

The Freewheelers don't cruise down the grade without their brakes. They're singles, often not by choice, who want to continue the *movanner* life style. I've traveled alone by auto in New Zealand. I was single, not by choice, for a few years. The best thing for me was to just keep moving. My grown kids didn't think much of the idea, but who listens to their kids? It's payback time for their teenage years.

For me to *movan* alone in New Zealand, I'd need a smaller van so I wouldn't have to rely on someone to help me in and out of blind spots, but I'd never feel alone or vulnerable. A small van or Class C *in good nick* could be picked up for a reasonable price. Check out the classifieds in *The Motor Caravanner*. At the end of your stay, leave it with a dealer and sell it, or trade up to something a little more exotic. If you don't want to travel alone, persuade a buddy to go with you. You'll find out in a hurry if you get along. That's how Dave and I got together. I asked him to crew for me through the Everglades in Florida — I'm afraid of alligators.

If you're single, get that *bum* out of the chair and go for it. Contact NZMCA and ask for someone who can fill you in on the *Freewheelers*.

The 2003 National Moonshine Easter Rally was held at the Gore Town and Country Club and at the Gore (SI) *A & P Showgrounds*. Members enjoyed the top entertainment, trade shows and craft stalls. We usually miss the National Rally — we're heading home the first part of April.

It's fun to roam around and see new sights, but even more fun to meet new people and join their lifestyle.

> **Warning**: If you play a small instrument, don't leave home without it.
>
> Practice up on your *Ghost Riders in the Sky* dance.

And this is where you snap in that well-worn *Lord of the Rings* tape, settle back, and figure out how you're going to do it.

DICTIONARY

Kiwis speak English — sort of. It's a kind of shorthand that's hard to follow. Here are a few words and phrases to get you warmed up so you can pretend you know what in the world they're talking about.

A & P Showgrounds: Agricultural & Pastoral Society. Like our state and county fairgrounds. Shops and offices close for Show Day — usually Friday of a three day show.

AA District Maps: Those free maps given out by the Automobile Association.

affair: Not the spicy kind with a little slap and tickle. A party.

All Whites: National Soccer Team.

All Blacks: National Rugby Team. A big deal in New Zealand. Similar to our football without the pads and helmets — just big big men in skinny little shorts and jerseys. Gridiron — for sissies I'm told by my Kiwi friend — is our football.

Anzac Day: At Gallipoli in World War I, the combined Australian and New Zealand forces (ANZAC) fought the Turks for eight and a half months. There were 213,980 Commonwealth casualties that touched the lives of almost every New Zealand family. This public holiday honors their heroism. Visit the Waeroa Army Museum to understand what these men endured.

aubergine: eggplant

bach: Weekend cottage in the North Island. Usually on the coast, near a lake, or in the mountains.

bangers: Sausages — not very spicy ones either. Often grilled and wrapped in a slice of white bread. If you want a little taste in your banger, find a Mexican chorizo in the butchery. An alpine stick is an extra long hot dog. A hot dog is a banger on a stick covered with batter and fried then dipped in tomato sauce.

barbe/barbie: A barbeque. You can also be invited to a barbe.

bathroom: Room with a bathtub and sink. If you're not interested in washing up, better ask for the toilet, lav or loo.

baths: Swimming pools or swimming baths.

bed clothes: What the bed wears — sheets and blankets.

beer: Brands seem to change with the districts. Move around enough, you'll get to sample some pretty good, some not so good beer.

beetroot: Red beets.

bench: Kitchen counter.

bickies: Biscuits. Can be crackers or cookies.

big bickies: You're in the money.

biscuit: Dry biscuits are crackers, sweet biscuits are cookies.

bloody: Universal adjective for just about anything. Often used when talking about the British. There're plenty of British running around New Zealand but I don't call them the Bloody British.

bonnet: Hood of a movan or car.

boot: Trunk of a car or in our case, a tacked-on wooden afterthought.

bottle store: Liquor store or package store.

bowser: Not a dog. It's a petrol pump.

Boxing Day: The day the family gets together to settle old scores. Not really. Just the day after Christmas. I asked once and was told, "It's the day we undo our Christmas boxes." There must be a better explanation.

brolly: Umbrella

brown eye: If some one gives you the brown eye, they've dropped their tweeds or mooned you.

bubble & squeak: Vegetable hash.

buggered: Clapped out, puffed, stonkered, worn out.

bum: What you sit on.

bush: The woods.

butchery: Butcher Shop.

Cabbage Tree: No. You can't pick cabbage off trees in New Zealand. The Ti Tree or Cabbage Tree has creamy-white flower heads in late spring. *Mobile New Zealand Native Trees* by Nancy M. Adams can help you identify these unusual native trees.

call: Come in person. It doesn't mean pick up the telephone.

Can I knock you up for breakfast?: Do you need a wakeup call?

capsicum: Sweet bell pepper.

caravan: A travel trailer — usually not a very fancy one, either.

carbonettes: Briquets.

cassia: Cinnamon. Cinnamon is sold but doesn't have the punch of cassia.

casual meal: If you ask for a seating at a hotel restaurant, you'll be asked if you're, "in house or casual." If you're not a registered guest, you're casual.

caught short: In a hurry to use the loo. This shouldn't be a problem. All towns, even small ones, have clean, convenient public facililties.

Certificated Member: A Certificated Member of NZMCA is entitled to join the Group Insurance Scheme.

champers: Champagne or bubbly.

cheerios: Not the little round O's that float in your milk — cocktail frankfurters.

cheesehead: A Green Bay Packer's fan? No. A Dutchman.

chemist shop: Drugstore.

chilly bin: Portable cooler or coolibah.

chip: A punnet, pottle, or small box of berries.

chippies: Potato chips.

chips: French fries.

chocka: What your movan will get when you start hauling goodies to take home — stuffed or filled.

chook: Chicken.

city: Town with more than 20,000 inhabitants.

Clapped out: Worn out.

COF: (Certificate of Fitness) Necessary before licensing vehicles with a gross laden weight over 3500 kg. Available from Vehicle Testing New Zealand Stations (LTSA) or a Private Testing Agency.

college: Most colleges are high schools. Teachers are trained at the College of Education.

convert a car: Convert a car and win a free trip to gaol — steal.

courgette: zucchini.

cracker: Could be from Georgia. Something really good — a corker. A female, a car, or anything you appreciate.

crib: Weekend cottage in the South Island.

cream: More like whipping cream. Watch what you buy. Kiwi's dump milk in their coffee and tea. If you want black tea or coffee, ask before it's served.

crook: You can go crook if the flu hits. Or, your movan can go crook if you forget to check the oil — then you'll really go crook — angry.

crumpet: English Muffin or a pretty young girl — sweet and tasty but kind of an airhead.

cuppa: You'll get invited to share a "cuppa" often. Can be tea or coffee.

dairy: Mom and Pop store, usually open seven days a week, that sells dairy products, bread, veges, and newspapers.

Dallie: Not a spotted dog. Dalmatians or Yugoslavs came to work the gum fields. You'll find Sons of Dalmatia Social Halls in the North Island.

dear: Pricy or expensive.

diddle: Swindle.

do a foreignie: Do your personal work on company time or with company money.

DOC: (Department of Conservation Te Papa Atawhai) Doc manages land and wildlife, promotes conservation and protects endangered species.

dog ranger: Dog catcher. He'll seldom run into a strong-eyed bitch — a working female who controls herds of cattle or flocks of sheep or geese by crouching down and staring at them. Ladies, try this with your husband — you're bound to get his attention.

dole: Unemployment. Based on the number of children in the family.

domain: Local park.

double: 6677 isn't six, six, seven, seven. It's double six, double seven. 888 is triple eight.

drapery: Where you go to get draped — a dry goods store.

draught beer: Tap brew or beer.

driver: That's not the engineer on that locomotive — he's the locomotive driver.

dustman: Garbage Collector — a FAST garbage collector. He gets paid by the street, not the hour.

face flannel: Face cloth, wash cloth.

facilities: Toilet sink and shower facililties.

fanny: Watch yourself with this one. It's not your bum or backside, it's the female frontside you usually don't talk about in polite conversation.

Farm Parks: Coastal land farmed by Department of Land & Survey where you can watch everyday life on a working farm.

fire: An electric heater is an electric fire.

fizzler: Failure or something that fizzled out.

fizzy drink: Soft drink.

flaming: Damned or bloody.

Forest Park: State Park.

Freedom Camping: Boondocking.

Freewheelers: One of the many special Interest Groups of NZMCA — for singles who enjoy the movanner lifestyle.

gallon: An Imperial gallon is bigger than the US gallon. An Imperial gallon is 1.19 US gallons. Petrol and diesel are sold by the litre, so don't worry about it.

gallops: Racing where the rider sits ON the horse. At the trots, the driver is pulled in a small cart — sulky. The trots can also be our backdoor trots.

gas: Don't ask for gas or you might get some. Ask for petrol at a petrol station and the attendant will fill your movan from the petrol bowser. Gas is what you get when you break wind or it could be LPG (Liquid Petroleum Gas) — which you'll need to run your movan's stove and refrigerator. Natural gas is used in homes for heating and cooking.

get your knickers in a twist: Get upset.

give it a go: Try it.

give it a miss: No thanks.

globe: A light bulb — usually with a bayonet base.

go like the clappers: What you do if a Jersey bull chases you.

Godzone: New Zealand is often called Godzone (God's own) country.

good on you: Good for you.

grammar school: High School.

greaseproof paper: Waxed paper.

greenstone: Native New Zealand Nephrite Jade. Used for Maori ornaments and tourist gifts.

grill: What you do with your meat and veges — usually on the barbe. Mixed grill is sausage, chops, beef, veges and chips.

grizzler: Complainer, whiner.

GST: (Goods and Service Tax) A 12.5% sales tax on almost every financial transaction, even labor charges — so quit complaining about our taxes.

gumboots: Calf-high black rubber boots you see Kiwi's wearing everywhere. They even manage to dance in them. Probably called gumboots because the were worn by the gum diggers who dug up the solidified golden sap of the Kauri tree. Handy to wear in a boggy paddy.

Guernsey: A football shirt or a good looking cow.

Group Insurance Scheme: NZMCA's insurance policy for motorcaravans.

hurricane hole: Where you anchor or tie up to get away from a hurricane.

haka: A Maori ceremonial dance for just about any reason — a birth, a marriage, a death.

hangi: A Maori barbeque which isn't cooked on a barbe. Kumara, veges, fish and what ever's on special at the butchery is wrapped in muslin, leaves or foil and lowered into a pit over hot rocks then doused with water, covered with dirt and left to steam for six to eight hours.

have a go at it: Try it.

hogget: A young sheep under two years of age.

honesty box: Set up at produce stands or golf courses. Drop in your fee for a round of golf or pick your fruits and veges and drop in your coins.

hooker: Not a fancy lady — just one of those big men in the little shorts who hang out on the All Black Team and play in the front row.

hoon: Teenage hooligan.

hot points: 220 volt, 50 cycle electrical outlets. Each has its own switch. You plug into the mains — the electrical wiring.

hubo: Distance measurement attached to the hub of a vehicle

ice blocks: Ice cubes or popsicles.

In good nick: In good shape.

Inland Revenue: Internal Revenue.

Iwi: Maori tribe or people.

jandels: Flip-flops. Pretty standard fashion accessory for a Kiwi.

jersey: Sweater. Could be a cardie, pullover, or a twin set.

judder bars: Speed bumps.

Jumper: Pullover

K's: Kilometers

Kauri: Straight, tall hardwood trees. In 1820 the HMS Coromandel came seeking trees for British masts and New Zealand was never the same. Sawpits, driving dams and later logging railroads were built. Most of the Kauri forests went up in smoke when the farmer's burns got out of control.

knackered: Worn out, beat.

kumara: Sweet potato brought to New Zealand by the Maori.

laundrette: Laundromat

licensed hotel: Hotel with a liquor license. A private hotel serves food but not alcohol.

litre: 1.057 US quarts or .88 Imperial quarts. Beer and petrol are sold by the litre.

lollies: Candy — any kind of candy.

loo: Toilet. Sometimes off by itself and not in the bathroom.

LPG: (Liquid Petroleum Gas) runs your movan's heater, refrigerator and stove as well as some cars. We had a van for a while which ran cheaply on LPG. We just pulled in to a separate bowser at the petrol station.

Maori: Pronounced Maw-ri or Ma-o-ri. Maori legends claims these Polynesian arrived in New Zealand in the 10th century. As they had no written language, it's hard to prove one way or the other. They speak of the "Great Migration" of the 14th century when they arrived from the Society Islands (Hawaiiki) eager to escape food shortages and war. There was plenty of food, though not much good red meat. About 40 tribes scattered around New Zealand and set up Pas — fortified villages — mostly in the warm North Island where their kumara liked the sun. They were not vegetarians. Tough Old Lady Cove reminds us what can happen to a nagging mother-in-law.

marae: Maori ceremonial ground and meeting house.

marmite: A flavored fortified yeast extract which is spread on bread. If you have a strong stomach, try some. I haven't tried Vegemite. Maybe it's the vege version.

marrow: Squash.

Members Discount Camp: Motorcamp offering a discount to NZMCA members.

metal: A metal road is gravel. Grades I & II are sealed.

milkbar: Mom and Pop store that sells ice cream, milkshakes, magazines and newspapers.

milk coffee: Coffee made with hot milk.

mince: Steak mince is ground beef ONLY.

moggy: A cat — a BIG cat. Most New Zealand cats are pretty hefty.

motorcamp: Where you park your movan, pitch a tent, or rent a cabin or caravan.

motorway: Freeway. There are some — usually around the larger cities.

mozzie: Those little biting buggers we call mosquitos.

muck around: Fart arse around or fool around.

mudguard: Fender.

muslin: Gauze for bandages.

motorcaravan: Self-propelled caravan.

nappies: Baby diapers. Don't ask for a napkin — you want a serviette.

National Parks: National Parks are managed by DOC. A domain is usually in the country. Cities and towns do not have parks, they have reserves. A park is where you park your car. Confused? Me, too.

next: The one after next. Not this coming Thursday — the following Thursday.

nick: Don't try this. Nick is to steal. If you nick something you'll be nicked and end up in the nick. Nick also means naked. Who wants to be nick in the nick?

Nippon Clipon: The Auckland bridge was once four lanes — now it's eight. The extra four were built in Japan, towed to Auckland and clipped on to the existing bridge.

no tipping: Means no dumping garbage. There's no tipping for services, either. GST is usually included in the menu price so — what you see is what you pay.

northerly: A warm wind from the north.

Northland: One of the 25 NZMCA membership areas. Northland has a sub-tropical climate with deep sea fishing.

number plate: License plate.

O.E. Overseas experience. Many young Kiwis take a trip overseas before settling down to raise a family and start a career.

one off: One of a kind.

ONO: In advertisements, it means "or near offer."

Op Shop: Opportunity Shop, Thrift Shop.

OZ: Land of the Aussies on the other side of the Tasman Sea.

paddock: Paddy or field.

Pakeha: White man, European.

panel beater: Where you take your movan when you ding your mudguard.

pavlova: Pav or Pavlova is the National Dessert. Aussies claim they, not the Kiwis, invented this concoction of meringue, whipped cream, strawberries and passion fruit. I can't see what all the fuss is about.

pavement: Sidewalk — not a paved road.

peter: Half gallon bottle of beer.

petrol: Gasoline. Sold by the litre.

phone box: Phone booth. And watch the numbers on the dial. They got scrambled up. Don't try to dial in the dark.

pie-cart: A traveling kitchen in a caravan with a flip down side. Enjoy fish and chips or anything fattening and fried.

pikelets: Small pancakes, usually cold, topped with jam or whipped cream.

Plunket Room: I saw these all through New Zealand and wondered if they were gambling parlors or some fun organization I was missing. Here, Mums can plunk down the baby for a free exam by the Plunket Nurse.

116

pokies: One-armed bandits, slot machines. Some are designated for the Cancer Society or other non-profit organization. Not a bad idea. If you want to donate your money, choose your favorite charity.

Pom: A bloody Englishman.

Post Shop: Post Office.

POP: (Park Over Property) Free or low cost parking for NZMCA members.

pudding: Anything sweet at the end of the meal. Dessert is usually fruit with or without cream drizzled over the top.

punga: A tree fern that looks like a small palm. Trunks are used for retaining walls.

raspberry bun: A hotdog bun covered with raspberry frosting.

reserve: A park — usually in a town or city.

Road User Charge: All diesel powered vehicles on the public roads must pay road user charges. Vehicles over 3500kg regardless of fuel type are required to have a RUC license. Movans usually have a distance license. Charges depend on axle configuration and weight of vehicle. Licenses are bought in multiples of 1000 k's.

rock melon: Cantaloupe. Not a very good one, either — usually too ripe and too mushy.

Roo bars: Brush guards. I don't know why they're called Roo bars. There're no kangaroos in New Zealand.

RSA: (Returned Servicemen's Association) Social clubs in most towns. Drop in for a good meal, good drinks and some good live entertainment.

salt and pepper shakers: Watch them. No they won't hop up and nip your nose, but the shaker with one hole or very few holes is the salt. The shaker with all the holes is the pepper.

Saturday paper: I only found one Sunday paper. You know, the thick one stuffed with ads and the comics — enough to keep you busy all day. The daily papers put out a fat Saturday paper then take Sunday off.

scone: Baking powder biscuit.

script: A prescription.

Sealed Road: Paved road.

self-contained van: A self-contained van can meet the sanitary needs of the occupants for a minimum of three days without discharging any waste.

shout: If a Kiwi shouts you a drink, he buys you a drink.

silverbeet: Swiss chard.

singlet: Sleeveless undershirt.

slap and tickle: This one can get you in the family way.

slip: A slide that blocks the road. Usually after a storm.

solicitor: Not a shady lady, just an attorney. Backroom lawyers are solicitors, courtroom lawyers, barristers.

southerly: A cold wind that comes in from the Antarctic.

spanner: Wrench.

speedo: Speedometer.

strawbs: Strawberries.

supper: A late night snack — not dinner.

sweets: Dessert.

swede: Rutabaga.

switches: Light or appliance switches. Remember, flip them up to turn them off.

take-aways: Food to go that you take away.

tea: Can be a tea or coffee break or the evening meal. The first time we were invited to tea, we ate a sandwich since we weren't quite sure what to expect. Big mistake. It was a full course meal ending with fruit and cream.

telly: Television.

tickle the peter: Don't get caught doing this, either. Keep your hands out of the cash register.

Tiki: Maori good luck charm sold in most shops. Usually carved from greenstone.

Tiki tour: Mini tour.

tip: The dump.

togs: Bathing togs or bathing suit.

torch: Flashlight.

tourist overstayer: Someone who hangs around illegally after their visa expires.

tramp: Hike, trek.

Travel Directory: NZMCA's Travel Directory lists dump stations, Park Over Properties, Free and Low Cost Parking and Member Discount Camps.

tuatara: A dinosaur-like lizard said to be 100 million years old. Some are alive and well in many museums.

Ugg Boots: Ugg for ugly, but who cares. Mid-calf length sheepskin boots with the fuzzy side turned in. You don't have to take a trip to New Zealand to buy a pair, just contact Classic Sheepskins in Napier.

valuer: NZMCA approved movan valuers are listed in the Handbook.

veges/veggies: Vegetables.

vermin: Rats, deer, opossum. Almost anything that doesn't have feathers.

Waitangi Day: A national holiday to celebrate the signing of the Treaty of Waitangi between Queen Victoria's government and some tribal chiefs on February 6, 1840. It has never been ratified, but it's still a day to kick back and enjoy the celebrations.

Warrant of Electrical Fitness: Required by law for motorcaravans to be connected to a 230 volt electrical system. Valid for four years from January of the year of issue.

weather: Weather is forecasted in degrees centigrade, so you have to multiply Celsius x 1.8 +32 for Farenheit. Don't bother. The weather forecast is usually wrong, anyway.

weta: A large scary-looking cricket who thinks you're large and scary.

windscreen: Windshield

wine biscuit: Doesn't taste like wine. Just another cookie. Maybe you dip it in wine.

WOF: (Warrant of Fitness) Necessary before licensing vehicles with a gross laden weight under 3500 kg.

wop-wops: Backwoods, boondocks.

zippers: Gentlemen — watch your zippers. No. They don't zip from top to bottom — they zip up the opposite side. Might want to brush up on your zipping skills in private.

And now I'll tell you. The 26th letter of the alphabet is pronounced zed, not zee. In New Zealand, this book is pronounced **RV in N Zed**. I think I like it better my way.

FOR MORE INFORMATION

I never promised you a travel guide — and you didn't get one. For a good travel guide, try *Moon Handbooks New Zealand* by Jane King and Andrew Hempstead. I'm only trying to get you wound up so you'll get there. *Moon Handbooks New Zealand* can tell you what you'll find once you get there. www.moon.com.

Tourist Information
   Jasons Travel Guides and Route Planner
   www.jasons.co.nz
   Tourism New Zealand
   www.purenz.co.nz

Regional Tourism Organisations — North Island
   Northland
   www.northland.org.nz
   Kauri Coast
   www.kauricoast.co.nz
   Auckland
   www.aucklandnz.co.nz
   Coromandel

www.thecoromandel.co.nz
Gisborne and Eastland
www.gisbornenz.co.nz
Rotorua
www.rotoruanz.co.nz
Hawkes Bay
www.hawkesbaynz.co.nz
Lake Taupo
www.laketauponz.co.nz
Waikato Region
www.waikatonz.co.nz
Wellington
www.wellingtonnz.co.nz

Regional Tourism Organisations — South Island
West Coast
www.west-coast.co.nz
Central South Island
www.southisland.org.nz
Central Otago
www.tco.org.nz
Queenstown
www.queenstown-nz.co.nz
Mount Cook
www.mtcook.org.nz
Christchurch and Canterbury
www.christchurchnz.net.nz
Southland
www.southland.org.nz

Campervan Rental
Adventure Deluxe Motorhomes
www.nzmotorhomes.co.nz
Britz

www.britz.co.nz
Kea Campers
www.keacampers.co.nz
Maui
www.maui-rentals.co.nz

Motorcaravan Parks
Holiday Accomodation Parks of NZ
www.hapnz.co.nz
Top 10 Holiday Parks
www.top10.co.nz

Government
Department of Conservation
www.doc.gov.nz
Land Transport Safety Authority
www.ltsa.gov.nz
New Zealand Immigration Service
www.immigration.gov.nz

Transportation and Tours
Flying Kiwi's Wilderness Expeditions
www.flyingkiwi.co.nz
Fullers
www.fullers.co.nz
InterCity Coachlines
www.intercitycoach.co.nz
Interisland Line
www.interislandline.co.nz
Magic Travellers Network
www.magicbus.co.nz
Tranz Rail
www.tranzrail.co.nz

Recreation
    Federated Mountain Clubs of New Zealand
    www.fmc.org.nz
    Fish and Game
    www.fishandgame.org.nz
    Forest & Bird
    www.forest-bird.org.nz
    New Zealand Alpine Club
    www.nzalpine.org.nz
    New Zealand Golf Club Directory
    www.nzgolfclubs.co.nz
    New Zealand Heritage Trails
    www.heritagetrails.org.nz.
    New Zealand Recreational Canoeing Association
    www.rivers.org.nz
    New Zealand Recreational Fishing Website
    www.fishing.net.nz

Especially for Movaners
    New Zealand Automobile Association
    www.nzaa.co.nz
    New Zealand Motor Caravan Association
    www.nzmca.org.nz
    E-mail: Enquiries@nzmca.org.nz
    Campervan and Motorhome Club of Australia
    www.cmca.net.au
    E-mail: Enquiries@cmca.net.au
    Vanco New Zealand
    E-mail: vanconz@ihug.co.nz

Newspapers
    New Zealand Herald
    www.herald.co.nz

INDEX

ORDER FORM

RV in NZ makes a great gift. It's filled with helpful information so you can spend your winters Freedom Camping south, way south, in New Zealand.

Please send me ____ copies @ $17.00 plus $3.00 for postage and handling (add only $1.00 postage for every added copy).

Name _____
(Please print)

Address_____

_____

City _____

State _____ Zip _____

Send check or money order to:

Marble Mountain Press
PMB214, 2019 Aero Wy, St 103
Medford, Oregon 97504
www.rvinnz.com

THANK YOU!